Moneybags Must Be So Lucky

Moneybags Must Be So Lucky

On the Literary Structure of *Capital*

Robert Paul Wolff

The University of Massachusetts Press

Amherst

1988

Copyright © 1988 by The University of Massachusetts Press

All rights reserved

Printed in the United States of America

LC 87–20580

ISBN 0–87023–615–6 (cloth); 616–4 (paper)

Set in Linotron Basilia Haas at Keystone Typesetting

Printed by Cushing-Malloy and bound by John Dekker & Sons

Library of Congress Cataloging-in-Publication Data

Wolff, Robert Paul.

Moneybags must be so lucky : on the literary structure of Capital

/ Robert Paul Wolff.

p.   cm.

ISBN 0–87023–615–6 (alk. paper). ISBN 0–87023–616–4

(pbk. : alk. paper)

1. Marx, Karl, 1818–1883.—Kapital. 2. Marx, Karl, 1818–1883.—

Kapital—Style. 3. Capital. I. Title.

HB501.M37W64 1988

335.4′1—dc19   87–20580

CIP

British Library Cataloguing in Publication data are available

For Susie

my once and future love

In order to be able to extract value from the consumption of a commodity, our friend, Moneybags, must be so lucky as to find, within the sphere of circulation, in the market, a commodity, whose use-value possesses the peculiar property of being a source of value, whose actual consumption, therefore, is itself an embodiment of labour, and, consequently, a creation of value. The possessor of money does find on the market such a special commodity in capacity for labour or labour-power.

Capital,
volume one, chapter 6,
"The Buying and Selling of Labour-Power"

Contents

Moneybags Must Be So Lucky

Introduction

These reflections on the relation between the literary form and philosophical message of *Capital* were originally delivered at the Amherst campus of the University of Massachusetts as the Romanell–Phi Beta Kappa Lectures for 1984–85. In their present form, they constitute the second of what will eventually be a trio of books devoted to a reinterpretation of Marx's great work. The entire undertaking dates from the late 1970s, when I began an attempt at interpretation and understanding that has occupied most of my scholarly attention for the past decade.

I had read volume one of *Capital* in 1957 as a graduate student and, like most progressive intellectuals of the sixties, I had pored over the early humanist writings—the *1844 Manuscripts,* the *German Ideology,* "On the Jewish Question," and so forth. I even considered myself some sort of socialist, though what that meant was a bit unclear to me. But the opening chapters of *Capital* had mystified me, and I accepted, unthinking, the received opinion that Marx was something of a crackpot when it came to economic theory.

Then, in the fall of 1976, I offered a graduate seminar called "Classics of Critical Social Theory" and, as an act of bravado, assigned *Capital,* volume one, to open the course. Almost from the first moment that I began to read through the text, as preparation for teaching, I was seized by a vision of Marx's enterprise that has guided my investigations ever since. As I worked through the extraordinary first chapter on value, with its bizarre mixture of classical economics and Hegelian metaphysics, couched in a bitterly satirical language quite unlike anything I had encountered elsewhere in political philosophy or the social sciences, I became more and more powerfully convinced that Marx's abstract theories of price and exchange, his angry critique of the injustices of capitalism, his complex conception of the objectively mystified character of bourgeois social reality, and his richly metaphorical invocation of the religious, political, and literary images of the Western cultural tradition, were so integrally connected that each could be understood only in relation to all the others.

The first task confronting me was a serious engagement with the technicalities of Marx's economic theories, and in this I was lucky to have, ready to hand in the Economics Department of the University of Massachusetts, the largest collection of Marxist economists in North America. Guided by the reading suggestions and periodic explications of Sam Bowles, Herb Gintis, and others, I undertook to master at least the elements of the modern mathematical reinterpretation of Marx's economics that was being carried out by first-rate theoretical economists around the world.

My relationship to the literary side of the enterprise is different. I am not a student either of literary critical theory or of textual interpretation. My principal acquaintance with each came through my familiarity with the scholarly and critical work of my former wife, Professor Cynthia Griffin Wolff. One reviewer of this manuscript speculated about whether I was a naive reader or a sophisticated student of literary thinking, and ended by paying me the enormous, but unfortunately unjustified, compliment of assuming the latter. As a consequence, I engage from time to time in the critical equivalent of reinventing the wheel. For example, the extended remarks in the first lecture on the relationship of Plato to his several audiences replow ground long planted and harvested—some might even say exhausted—by the critical community.[1] Nevertheless, I have chosen to publish the text without a burdensome critical apparatus. My purpose is to attempt not merely to explicate Marx's text but also to reinvoke something of its affective power.

The third, or philosophical side, of the triangle was, as Eliza Doolittle would put it, mother's milk to me, and seemed to pose the most manageable challenge. Since that time, I have come to see that this last portion of the enterprise is actually the conceptually most problematic, requiring as it does a thorough sorting out of the long-debated issue of methodological individualism and the analysis of social reality.

I conceived the product of these investigations as a single lengthy volume in which I would exhibit the inner connection between the linear equations of Marxian value theory and the satiric thrust of Marx's literary invocations, all in the aid of explicating the objectively contradictory character of capitalist social reality in its ironic relation to those of us who strive to understand capitalism from within.

Fortunately, concerned friends called my attention to the fact that there is a very small audience indeed for a book that is part linear algebra, part literary criticism, and part methodology of the social sciences. Good sense prevailed, and I determined to recast my reading of *Capital* in three shorter volumes, each of which would be independently accessible to an appropriate audience. The first volume, devoted to the

1 See, for example, Peter J. Rabinowitz, "'What's Hecuba to Us?' The Audience's Experience of Literary Borrowing," in *The Reader in the Text,* ed. Susan R. Suleiman and Inge Crosman (Princeton: Princeton University Press, 1980).

mathematical reinterpretation of the economic theories, appeared several years ago.[2] With the publication of the present volume, there remains only the hardest part of the job to complete—the philosophical weaving together of the two in an explication of Marx's theory of social reality. Long experience has taught me not to make promises that I am uncertain to fulfill, but I can at least hope that the third volume will appear with no greater delay than has separated the first from the second.

There is, of course, nothing novel in construing *Capital* as a work of literary art, over and above its character as a work of theoretical economics. The first person to understand this was the author himself. He was notoriously dilatory about getting manuscript to the publisher, and for several years before the actual publication of volume one in 1867, his letters are full of predictions of its appearance, apologies for the delay, promises that it would be delivered to the printer, and even, if I interpret one letter correctly, wagers with Engels.[3] In a letter of 31 July 1865, Marx offers the following justification to Engels for the delay in publishing the work that had already taken him so long to complete:

> Now as concerns my work, I will pour out for you some pure wine [a reference to Engels's remark about the twelve bottles, quoted in footnote 3]. There are still three chapters to write in order to complete the theoret-

2 Robert Paul Wolff, *Understanding Marx: A Reconstruction and Critique of* Capital (Princeton: Princeton University Press, 1984).

3 I have in mind Engels's letter to Marx of 15 July 1865, in which he remarks at one point, apropos Marx's delay in completing volume one, that "Sept. 1 was the absolutely final deadline, and is costing twelve bottles of wine, as you know." *Marx-Engels Werke* (Berlin: Dietz Verlag, 1965), B. 31, S. 129. Engels uses the phrase "Ultimatissimal-Termin," which appears to be a humorous mixture of Latin, English, and German.

ical part (the first three books). Then there is still the fourth book, the historical-literary one, to write, which is for me relatively the easiest part, inasmuch as all the problems have been solved in the first three books, this last being therefore more a repetition in historical form. But I cannot bring myself to send off anything before the whole lies before me. Whatever shortcomings they may have, [this phrase is in English in the original—ed.], the merit of my writings is that they are an artistic whole, and that is only attainable by my method, never to allow them to be printed before they lie before me as a *whole*.[4]

To be sure, this passage can be construed as nothing more than a dilatory author's excuse, but it provides a hook on which to hang a literary reading of *Capital,* and as such is taken by me with the utmost seriousness.

Perhaps the first literary critic to offer an extended analysis and appreciation of Marx's literary style is Edmund Wilson, in his classic study of the socialist tradition, *To the Finland Station.*[5] Wilson was a consummate reader of texts, and he was fully aware of the ironic character of Marx's communications in the opening chapters of *Capital.* Unfortunately, Wilson was much less in control of Marx's economic theories, with the result that he is unable finally to tell us why Marx should have chosen to write as he did. Nevertheless, his discussion is well worth excerpting at length.

Another element of Marx's genius is a peculiar psychological insight: no one has ever had so deadly a sense of

4 Ibid., S. 132. In my translation, I follow the translation of Dona Torr in *Marx and Engels: Selected Correspondence, 1846–1895* (New York: International Publishers, 1942), 204.

5 Edmund Wilson, *To the Finland Station* (1940; reprint, New York: Doubleday, Anchor Books, 1955).

the infinite capacity of human nature for remaining oblivious or indifferent to the pains we inflict on others when we have a chance to get something out of them for ourselves.

In dealing with this theme, Karl Marx became one of the great masters of satire. Marx is certainly the greatest ironist since Swift, and he has a good deal in common with him. Compare the logic of Swift's "modest proposal" for curing the misery of Ireland by inducing the starving people to eat their surplus babies with the argument in defense of crime which Marx urges on the bourgeois philosophers (in the so-called fourth volume of *Das Kapital*): crime, he suggests, is produced by the criminal just as "the philosopher produces ideas, the poet verses, the professor manuals," and practising it is useful to society because it takes care of the superfluous population at the same time that putting it down gives employment to many worthy citizens. . . .

Improving on Sir Thomas More, who, at an earlier stage of capitalist development, at the time when the great estates were being depopulated and turned into sheep-runs, had said that the sheep were eating the people—Marx presents us with a picture of a world in which the commodities command the human beings. . . .

[And finally:]

Marx . . . loves his abstractions. . . . A good deal of this part of *Das Kapital* is gratuitous and simply for show. . . . But the chief value of these abstract chapters which alternate with the chapters of history is—in the first volume, at any rate—an ironic one. . . . The meaning of the impersonal-looking formulas which Marx produces with so scientific an air is, he reminds us from time to time as if casually, pennies withheld from the worker's pocket, sweat squeezed out of his body, and natural enjoyments denied his soul. In competing with the pundits of economics, Marx has written something in the nature of a parody; and, once we have read *Das Kapital,* the conventional works on economics never seem the same to us again: we can always see through their arguments and figures the realities of the crude human relations which it is their purpose or effect to mask.[6]

This is really quite wonderful—no one, I think, has written more intelligently on Marx's use of irony in the almost half century since Wilson first published his book. Nevertheless, much of the force of Wilson's insight is lost by his inability to connect it with the logic of Marx's argument. In Wilson's account, Marx becomes a brilliant satirist and ironist who, more or less superfluously or by mistake, filled his otherwise admirable diatribe with tedious economic abstractions. Only a few pages after he has paid Marx the unparalleled compliment of placing him at the pinnacle of satire with Swift, Wilson dismisses Marx's central theoretical ideas as "a creation of the metaphysician who never abdicated before the economist in Marx"[7]—"metaphysician" being taken here, we may be reasonably confident, as a term of opprobrium.

Now, it is true that even the greatest minds can exhibit a quirky respect for implausible ideas. One thinks of Newton on astrology, Berkeley on the virtues of tar water—Aquinas

6   Ibid., 290–93. The passage on the productive virtues of crime is in volume one of Karl Marx's *Theories of Surplus Value* ([vol. 4 of *Capital*], pt. 1, trans. Emile Burns. [Moscow: Progress Publishers, 1963]), in an addendum entitled "Digression (on productive labor)." Cf. *Marx-Engels Werke,* B. 26.1, S. 363.

7   Wilson, *Finland Station,* 298.

on God. But it is an odd sort of compliment to call a writer the greatest ironist since Swift, and then to adjudge his most serious intellectual efforts crackpot metaphysics. Surely, with admirers of that cast, Marx would have done better in the company of Nassau Senior!

This is not the place to argue the merits of Marx's economic theories. I hope that I have established, in the first part of this trilogy, precisely what can survive rigorous theoretical critique in Marx's labor theory of value, and what must be discarded or revised. But there remains an equally important question, which is the subject of the three lectures reproduced here: What is the logical connection between Marx's literarily brilliant ironic discourse and his "metaphysical" account of the nature of bourgeois social reality? Or, to pose the same question differently, Why *must* Marx write as he does if he is to accomplish the intellectual tasks he has set for himself? This volume is an attempt at an answer.

First, however, a few words should be said about efforts subsequent to Wilson's to come to terms with the literary merits of *Capital.* Perhaps the most substantial is the lengthy discussion by Stanley Edgar Hyman more than two decades after Wilson's book appeared.[8] Like Wilson, Hyman recognizes the literary qualities of *Capital.* In addition to demonstrating Marx's invocation of classical mythology, Hyman calls attention to the repeated use of the metaphor of stripping away of veils as a figure for the revelation of the ugly reality beneath the appealing appearances. Nevertheless, like Wilson, Hyman dismisses Marx's economic theories, remarking at one point apropos the relation between socialism and the labor theory of value that "all we need note here

8   Stanley Edgar Hyman, *The Tangled Bank: Darwin, Marx, Frazer and Freud as Imaginative Writers* (New York: Atheneum, 1962).

is that neither theory depends on the other, and that neither is refutable by observation in the market."[9]

All of this is quite helpful as general literary observation, but completely useless as an explanation of *why* Marx chose to write as he did. I am convinced that no engagement with *Capital* as "imaginative literature"[10] can be of any real use in the understanding of that text unless it is informed by a sophisticated contemporary grasp of the analytics of Marx's political economy. Karl Marx was indeed the greatest ironist since Swift, and *Capital* is powerful imaginative literature, but Marx was, *at the very same time, and in the very same texts,* a brilliant theoretical economist, who was convinced that imaginative writing was the best way to communicate his theoretical insights.

A good deal more suggestive is the work of a Mexican critic of Marx, Ludovico Silva, whose short book, *El Estilo Literario de Marx,* contains a number of useful observations about the structure and function of Marx's irony.[11] In the concluding chapter, "Epilogo sobre la Ironia y la Alienacion," Silva plays on the etymological meaning of "metaphor" as a translation, or movement away from, to argue that all of capitalist society is a metaphor, a displacement of human life away from its real sense toward a distorted sense. Alienation, he suggests, is *the* capitalist metaphor. In capitalism, there is a translation or movement away from reality to the monstrous, from use value to exchange value, from quality or quantity. It is this structural fact about capitalism that explains Marx's adoption of ironic discourse, Silva argues.

9   Ibid., 127–28.
10   Ibid., 133.
11   Ludovico Silva, *El Estilo Literario de Marx* (Mexico: Siglo XXI Editores, S. A., 1971). See esp. 116–30. My special thanks to Alex Pienknagura, who translated portions of the text for me.

All of this is extremely helpful, I think, both as literary insight into Marx's text, and as a clue to the objective structure of capitalism. My analyses, especially in the second and third lectures, develop interpretations parallel to those of Silva in a number of respects.

One

The Ontological Presuppositions of Literary Style

To read the opening chapters of *Capital* is to be plunged into an extraordinary literary world, quite unlike anything in the previous, or indeed subsequent, history of political economy. The text is rich in literary and historical allusions to the entire corpus of Western culture. The argument is twisted, obscure, convoluted, and terribly difficult to follow. Marx invokes religious images, Mephistophelean images, political images. He writes now mockingly and scornfully, now soberly and with proper professorial seriousness, now angrily and bitterly. He swings with baffling speed from the most abstruse metaphysical reflections to vividly sensual evocations of the sufferings and struggles of English workers against the oppressions of their bosses. At one instant he is a polemicist, writing to the moment. At the next, he is a pedant, calling down authorities in six languages from twenty centuries to confirm his etymological tracings and analytical speculations.

What is going on? What possible purpose can Marx have in writing thus? How are we to respond to the text as readers, as interpreters, as social critics and political economists?

Needless to say, opinions differ. Louis Althusser, that most *raffiné* of French philosophical Marxists, recommends in his preface to the French edition of *Capital* that beginning readers skip the famous opening chapter on value, returning to it only after they have mastered the remainder of volume one. Modern mathematical Marxists ignore the text itself save for a sprinkling of selected quotations, in much the way that modern physicists ignore the text of Newton's *Principia* and Galileo's *Dialogue*. A number of contemporary authors strive to imitate the abstraction and obscurity, but not the wit and sensuous immediacy, of *Capital,* with results that are all too successful.

The majority opinion seems to follow what might be thought of as the public-health or childhood-polio interpretation of *Capital.* According to this reading, Karl Marx as a young man contracted a nearly fatal case of the particularly virulent strain of Hegelism that raged pandemically throughout Germany during the third and fourth decades of the nineteenth century. Although he somehow survived the illness, he was intellectually crippled for life. Hence it is simply bad manners to mock him as he drags himself painfully, awkwardly from concept to concept in the Realm of Ideas. Rather ought we to marvel that he can traverse the distance from the premises to the conclusion of an argument, and we ought scarcely to expect him to ascend a *ratiocinatio polysyllogistica* like Fred Astaire tip-tapping his way up a flight of stairs.

The British version of this rather curious literary theory simply has it that Marx was German, and hence could not be expected to achieve the clarity and simplicity of Locke, Hume, Smith, or Ricardo. A thinker reared on Hegel and Feuerbach has little chance of laying his thoughts before an audience in a discourse free of metaphysics. As Joan Robinson says, echoing the vulgar empiricism of the Viennese positivists:

No point of substance in Marx's argument depends upon the labour theory of value. Voltaire remarked that it is possible to kill a flock of sheep by witchcraft if you give them plenty of arsenic at the same time. The sheep, in this figure, may well stand for the complacent apologists of capitalism; Marx's penetrating insight and bitter hatred of oppression supply the arsenic, while the labour theory of value provides the incantations.[1]

Marx, we are to suppose, was a very angry, very confused man with "penetrating insight" and a "theory" that amounts to no more than incantation.

In the United States, Paul Samuelson's contemptuous dismissal of Marx as a "minor post-Ricardian" and an "autodidact" has, by and large, won the day, despite the efforts of such economists as Paul Baran and Paul Sweezy.

These views of Marx's literary efforts, one must insist at the outset, have a certain manifest implausibility. Karl Marx, as much as any philosopher who ever lived, was a man of the book. Despite the activist ring of the famous eleventh thesis on Feuerbach, he armed himself for his assault on bourgeois capitalist society and theory by a decade-long study of everything that had ever been written on political economy. Marx obviously conceived of *Capital* as his *hauptwerk,* his *Don Quixote,* his *Principles of Political Economy and Taxation,* his *Faust.* It was intended to be the work that would immortalize him, as indeed it has done.

This is, after all, the same Karl Marx who, twenty years earlier, had penned the blood-chilling lines of the *Communist Manifesto.* Say what you will about his theories, the man

---

1   Joan Robinson, *An Essay on Marxian Economics,* 2d ed. (London: Macmillan, 1966), 22.

could write. Is it plausible, is it even conceivable, that he would, absentmindedly as it were, begin his opus magnum with one hundred pages of clumsy confusion?

Nevertheless, the text confronts us in all its difficulty. Can we be certain that Marx could have laid his thoughts before us *à l'anglaise,* had he wished to? The answer is yes, and happily the evidence is available in one of the best-known and most widely read of Marx's shorter writings, a work furthermore that Marx actually composed in English. In the late spring of 1865, while he was, from the testimony of his letters, hard at work finishing and polishing the first volume of *Capital,* Marx was called upon to present a theoretical reply to several controversial theses advanced before the General Council of the First International by a member, John Weston. In two sessions, on 20 June and 27 June 1865, Marx read a discourse of roughly twenty thousand words. The first half of the piece is directed quite narrowly to Weston's theses, but midway through, Marx takes a breath and begins again. "Citizens," he says, "I have now arrived at a point where I must enter upon the real development of the question."[2] There then follows a brilliantly clear, compressed, utterly coherent summary of the theses of the opening portion of *Capital.*

The diction of *Value, Price, and Profit* is quite unlike that of the corresponding portions of *Capital.* Indeed, the style of the essay is almost indistinguishable from that of David Ricardo and the classical school against which Marx was arguing. Here he is, for example, explaining to his audience of British workmen that the value of a commodity is determined by the labor indirectly as well as directly required for its production:

2   Karl Marx, *Value, Price and Profit,* edited by his daughter Eleanor Marx Aveling (Chicago: Charles H. Kerr and Co., n.d.), 29.

In calculating the exchangeable value of a commodity we must add to the quantity of labour *last* employed the quantity of labour *previously* worked up in the raw material of the commodity, and the labour bestowed on the implements, tools, machinery, and buildings with which such labour is assisted. For example, the value of a certain amount of cotton yarn is the crystallisation of the quantity of labour added to the cotton during the spinning process, the quantity of labour previously realised in the cotton, itself, the quantity of labour realised in the coal, oil, and other auxiliary matter used, the quantity of labour fixed in the steam-engine, the spindles, the factory buildings, and so forth. Instruments of production properly so-called, such as tools, machinery, buildings, serve again and again for a longer or shorter period during repeated processes of production. If they were used up at once, like the raw material, their whole value would at once be transferred to the commodities they assist in producing. But as a spindle, for example, is but gradually used up, an average calculation is made, based upon the average time it lasts, and its average waste or wear and tear during a certain period, say a day.[3]

Compare this with the following passage, chosen virtually at random from the opening chapter of Ricardo's *Principles:*

Suppose the weapon necessary to kill the beaver [Ricardo is alluding to the famous example in chapter 6 of the first book of Adam Smith's *Wealth of Nations*] was constructed with much more labour than that necessary to kill the deer, on account of the greater difficulty of approaching near to the former animal, and the consequent necessity of its being more true to its mark: one

3   Ibid., 60–61.

beaver would naturally be of more value than two deer, and precisely for this reason, that more labour would, on the whole, be necessary for its destruction. Or suppose that the same quantity of labour was necessary to make both weapons, but that they were of very unequal durability: of the durable implement only a small portion of its value would be transferred to the commodity, a much greater portion of the value of the less durable implement would be realized in the commodity which it contributed to produce.[4]

Note Marx's use of "bestowed," which is Ricardo's term for the relationship of labor to the commodities produced with it. The passage by Marx could easily have found its way into the *Principles*. Later in the same section, Marx introduces the concept of money. "Price," he says, "is nothing but the *monetary expression of value.* . . . The value of gold and silver, like that of all commodities, is regulated by the quantity of labour necessary for getting them. . . . So far as it is but the monetary expression of value, price has been called *natural price* by Adam Smith, *prix nécessaire* by the French physiocrats."[5] After ridiculing the notion that all sellers of commodities, in general, can sell their wares for more than their value, Marx concludes the section by asserting flatly:

To explain, therefore, the *general nature of profit,* you must start from the theorem that, on an average, commodities are *sold at their real values,* and that *profits are derived from selling them at their values,* that is, in proportion to the quantity of labour realised in them. If you

4   David Ricardo, *Principles of Political Economy and Taxation,* ed. Piero Sraffa with the collaboration of M. H. Dobb (Cambridge: Cambridge University Press, 1951), 23.
5   Marx, *Value,* 35.

cannot explain profit upon this supposition, you cannot explain it at all.[6]

And so on and on. All of this, whether one considers it correct or incorrect as political economy, is as clear, as coherent, as unmetaphysical as the plainest-speaking English empiricist could want. Marx wrote this essay, let me repeat, in 1865, precisely when he was preparing volume one of *Capital* for the press. It simply will not do to suppose that the obscurities and vexations of the opening chapters of *Capital* are merely the inadequate expository efforts of a Hegelian metaphysician. Marx had some purpose in mind in choosing to write in a deliberately mystifying manner. We shall not truly understand *Capital* until we penetrate that purpose.

We seek to understand why Marx writes as he does, but a direct examination of the text does not immediately reveal the answer. I propose, therefore, to take a somewhat circuitous route, and begin by considering in a more general way the relationship between ontology and literary style—or, less pretentiously, the relationship between the style of a text and the nature of the object of its discourse. As Hume says in the *Treatise* as he begins his search for the idea of causal necessity, "We must, therefore, proceed like those, who being in search of any thing that lies conceal'd from them, and not finding it in the place they expected, beat about all the neighbouring fields, without any certain view or design, in hopes their good fortune will at last guide them to what they search for."[7]

Knowledge is the apprehension of the structure of some realm of being. Truth is the correspondence of thought and

6   Ibid., 37.
7   David Hume, *A Treatise of Human Nature*, ed. L. A. Selby-Bigge (Oxford: At the Clarendon Press, 1888), 77–78.

being. Thought takes form in language, and knowledge is expressed in judgments. If we are to have knowledge, therefore, the form of our language must in some way be adequate to the structure of the object of our knowledge. There must be available, in our language, formal possibilities corresponding to the possible structures of being. Otherwise, it will be impossible for us to express, and hence to know, some characteristics of the object of our knowledge.

Since I wish to argue that Marx's literary style constitutes a deliberate attempt to find the philosophically appropriate language for expressing the ontological structure of the social world, I propose to look at the relationship in general of language to being. Let me begin, somewhat implausibly, with a view concerning the nature and appropriate role of metaphor in language. This view finds expression in the poetry of the English metaphysical poets of the late sixteenth and seventeenth centuries. Although they did not themselves articulate a theory of their practice, contemporary continental critics, such as the Spaniard Emmanuele Tesauro, did. Let us ask on what ontology, or theory of the structure of being, this position is based, and what is thereby implied for the metaphorical use of language.

The metaphysical poets conceived of the universe as having been created by God in such a way, and according to such a plan, as to establish an endless series of correspondences or parallels among the most disparate elements of the creation. As the moon shines by the reflected light of the sun, so the subjects of a great monarch shine by his reflected glory, and so too does the lover live in light or shadow as his beloved bestows upon him the radiance of her smile. As the sun rises in the East, heralding the start of an earthly day, so the crucified Christ, God's Son, rose in the East to heaven, heralding thereby the dawn of a new day in the spiritual life of the world; so, eventually, do we hope to rise to heaven to begin the endless day that awaits us beyond the night of the grave.

These correspondences are in a manner of speaking metaphors, for they are comparisons of things superficially unlike, in whose structure and inner relationships we perceive formal parallels. The divine creation, according to the worldview implicit in metaphysical poetry, is through and through metaphorical. Joseph Mazzeo, in a classic essay on the subject, says this of Tesauro:

> Tesauro maintained that *"acutezze"* or conceits were not created by men only but by God, his angels, and by animals. The universe was created by a God who was a "witty creator," an *"arguto favellatore,"* a witty writer or talker. The world was a poem made up of conceits. The notion that the world is a poem of God is old enough as a conception and, in various forms, goes back at least to Plotinus. However, the important difference for Tesauro is that the world is a "metaphysical" poem and God a "metaphysical" poet. He conceived *"ingegno"* [i.e., ingenuity or wit] as the faculty in man analogous to God's creative power. It is a small particle of the divine nature, for it can create "being" where there was no "being" before. As God created a "metaphysical" world, so the poet creates "metaphysical" poems.[8]

John Donne gives voice to much the same view in his "Devotions on Emergent Occasions." "My *God,* my *God,* thou art a *direct God,* may I not say, a *literall God* . . . but thou art also . . . a *figurative,* a *metaphoricall God* too . . . Neither art thou thus a *figurative,* a *Metaphoricall God,* in thy *word* only,

---

8   Joseph A. Mazzeo, "Metaphysical Poetry and the Poetic of Correspondence," *Journal of the History of Ideas* 14 (1953): 228.

but in thy workes too. The *stile* of thy *works,* the *phrase* of Thine *Actions,* is *Metaphoricall . . .* This hath occasioned thine ancient *servants,* whose delight it was to write after thy *Copie,* to proceede the same way in their *expositions* of the *Scriptures,* and in their composing both of *publike liturgies,* and of *private prayers* to thee, to make their accesses to thee in such a kind of *language,* as thou wast pleased to speake to them, in a *figurative,* in a *Metaphoricall language.*"[9]

Tesauro was defending the rather baroque uses to which metaphor had been put, especially in pulpit oratory, and so his argument takes the form of a claim that metaphors are *appropriate,* given the nature of God's creation. But one could quite easily transform this into the more powerful and interesting claim that the poet, or the sermonizer, *must* use metaphor adequately to capture the structure of what God has made. As Mazzeo says, summarizing Tesauro's position: "God created a world full of metaphors, analogies, and conceits, and so far from being ornamentation, they are the law by which creation was effected. God wrote the book of nature in metaphor, and so it should be read."[10]

There is thus a correspondence between the metaphorical language of the poet and the metaphorical structure of creation—a metacorrespondence, as it were—relating the correspondences in nature to the correspondences in the metaphorical figures of the poem. In a manner of speaking, the poet *discovers* metaphors rather than inventing them, for the correspondences on which the metaphors rest lie ready in nature, their metaphysical or religious significance having been imparted to them by the supreme Word-Maker.

The poets claim only that metaphor is justified by the char-

9   John Donne, *Devotions Upon Emergent Occasions,* ed. Anthony Raspa (New York: Oxford University Press, 1987), 99–100.
10   Mazzeo, "Metaphysical Poetry," 229.

acter of the divine creation, or that metaphor enables the poet to touch the reader's feelings, or that an understanding of God's purpose is strengthened by metaphorical expression. But I think we can, without too great a distortion, take the further step, and argue that *only* metaphor can give adequate literary expression to the objective correspondences established by a witty or conceited creator.

The central point is the intentionality of the correspondences. God does not simply establish a proportionality between the relation of sun to moon and the relation of monarch to subject. He establishes an inner connection between the two which is a part of the meaning that he imposes on His Creation. Fully to understand the relation of sun to moon and king to subject is to understand not only that these are parallel, but also that they were intended to be parallel, and were intended each to refer to the other. A paratactic gloss of this conceit captures only a part of God's intention, namely the equality of ratios. It misses the overdetermination of relationships, through which the relationship of king to subject is apprehended *in* the relationship of sun to moon. Only a figure of speech equally overdetermined will express completely what God has intended by His divine Metaphor.

If one embraces the ontology of the metaphysical poets, then it follows that only metaphorical language is a suitable linguistic vehicle for expressing our apprehension of being. Our discourse must have available within it the literary resources required for articulating the correspondences that are an objective characteristic of the created universe. Just as the assertion of certain complex relationships of causal dependence and reciprocity requires syntactic resources of subordination and superordination in the construction of sentences, so the correct linguistic articulation of the overdetermined ratios of the created world requires metaphors that reflect, in our speech, the intentions and wit of the Creator.

There is one further point that will become centrally important later in our discussion, when we arrive finally at Marx. To say that a poet speaks metaphorically is to say that the poet sees certain resemblances or correspondences and wishes us to see them as well. But to say that the world is *in itself* metaphorical—so that the poet merely discovers what already exists—is to say that objects, events, and relationships *themselves* refer to other objects, events, and relationships. Now, on the face of it, the rising of the sun in the East cannot itself *refer to* the resurrection of Jesus, or the eventual ascension into heaven of those who have been saved, although I, as the observer of the event, may draw that comparison. Only if the universe is imbued with meaning, only, that is, if the universe is the intentional product of a purposeful Creator, can it make sense to describe objects or events as themselves referring.

This brief look at the worldview of the metaphysical poets has given us a particularly simple and elegant example of the way in which a conception of the structure of an object of discourse can shape, or even dictate, the literary devices by which we articulate that structure. We can take a long step toward an understanding of Marx's use of language, and its relationship to his theory of the structure of social reality, by exploring in greater detail the much more complicated interconnections among ontology, epistemology, psychology, and literary style in the Socratic dialogues of Plato.

Plato held that the goal of the philosopher is a rational understanding of the most fundamental principles that guide us when we reason, evaluate, and choose; that such an understanding is achieved by an unceasing process of critical self-examination; that the key to successful self-criticism is a rigorous and unflinching investigation of the distinction between appearance and reality; and that the appropriate vehicle for the conduct of this quest and the expression of its results is ironic discourse.

As Plato indicates in Socrates' autobiographical reminiscence in the *Phaedo,* Socrates quite early rejected the investigations of the cosmologists into physical nature, into the identity and mixture of the elements, and what today we would call the causes of things. His concern was with the moral realm, with principles of right reason, of just evaluation, of virtuous action. Consequently, he held, the truth must be sought within, for though a traveler from afar can inform us of the customs of strange peoples or the climate of distant lands, no one but I can look within me to discover the rules and standards, implicit or explicit, on which my judging, evaluating, and choosing rest.

Critical self-examination is the way to this truth. *Self-*examination, because the truth lies within, and *critical* self-examination because the aim is truth, not mere self-awareness. Once having identified a principle actually operative in my reasoning—what Kant two millennia later would call a "subjective maxim"—I must subject it to critique to determine whether it is indeed a principle to which I should give my assent. In the quest for rational self-knowledge, the wisdom of those who have gone before us cannot significantly ease the task of self-examination. At best, the wise philosopher can point the way and warn of pitfalls.

Self-examination proceeds, Socrates teaches, by an exploration in every possible sphere of the distinction between appearance and reality. The stick in water *appears* bent even though it is *really* straight. Reason enables us to overcome the misleading testimony of the senses. The sun *appears* larger when low in the sky, though we know it to be unchanged in size. The pain of a life-saving operation *appears* evil, although we know it to be necessary; and the pain of judicial correction, evil though it may *seem* to the ignorant, is (Plato argues) actually beneficial. The common opinion of the marketplace—that it is right to help one's friends and harm one's enemies—*appears* sound, but is in fact incoherent, being easily shown to lead to self-contradictory conclusions. Even the *apparent* happiness of the absolute tyrant is *actually* the most extreme misery, an obsessive distortion of the inner harmony of the soul.

Thus far Plato's doctrine is simple and straightforward enough, though he deepens it considerably by the elaborate ontological justification he offers for it in the theory of the forms. But now his thought becomes difficult and, for our purposes, important.

Suppose that I have been prone to reason from the premises "Some A are B" and "Some B are C" to the conclusion "Some A are C." This is, of course, a fallacious inference, and presumably either a bit of critical self-examination, or some instruction in elementary logic, will show me the error of my ways. Once I have achieved a clear understanding of the root of the fallacy, I cease to make such inferences. Indeed, I cease even to be *tempted* to make them. I simply recognize that premises of that form do not entail such a conclusion, and there the matter ends.

But even after I have come to understand the theory of refractive indices, so that I know, in some rationally coherent way, that the stick in water is not bent, and why nevertheless it looks bent, I still perceive it *as* bent. Somewhat more to the point, be my character ever so strong and my rational understanding of the principles of dental hygiene ever so sound, I continue to experience twinges of fear as I seat myself in the dentist's chair. The things of the physical world, the opinions of the multitude, the illicit pleasures of the unjust, never cease to *appear* real, true, or good to us, even after we have achieved that rational grasp of the distinction between appearance and reality from which vantage we know them to be mere appearances.

Let us pursue this matter of the bent stick. When I misconstrue a figure dimly glimpsed at dusk, mistakenly thinking it a man when it is merely a particular arrangement of shadows upon a bush, I confuse appearance with reality, to be sure. But there is no significant connection between what is truly there and what I mistook it for. There is no reason to suppose that any other observer will make just my mistake, for the error has arisen from an adventitious trick of the light, coupled perhaps with expectations and perceptual inclinations peculiar to me.

In the case of the stick, however, things are quite otherwise. When I look at the stick, I see it as bent, I know it to be straight, and (once I have learned the principles of optics) I understand why it must appear bent to me even though—or better, precisely because—it is straight. Furthermore, I know that it will look bent to other observers, and I know too what knowledge they shall have to gain before they understand, as I do, that it *is* straight and why it appears bent.

In all such cases (which are legion), the world comes to be divided into two sorts of people: one group, possibly rather small, who share our knowledge of the true situation, including our awareness that others will mistakenly think the stick to be bent; and a second, perhaps larger, group, who—living, as it were, at the level of appearances—will simply suppose that the stick is bent.

The problem confronted by Plato is how to give literary

expression to this ontologically, epistemologically, and psychologically complex situation. His answer is what we have come to know as Socratic irony.

Irony is a mode of communication that employs an utterance with a double meaning, to which correspond two audiences. The first, or superficial, audience understands only the apparent or superficial meaning, and thinks, wrongly, that it has understood the communication entire. The second, or real, audience understands both meanings, superficial and real, and understands as well that the first audience has misunderstood the utterance. Irony is thus a private joke between the speaker and the real audience, at the expense of the superficial or apparent audience. Hence the feeling of shared superiority engendered by irony.

For example, a naive speaker asks one philosopher, in the presence of a second, whether Albert Schweitzer was a great thinker. "Oh yes," the first philosopher replies, "he was a thinker universally admired!" The naive speaker takes this as a simple yes, and concludes that Schweitzer was indeed a great philosopher. But the second philosopher understands the reply as an ironic remark, the real meaning of which is that although outsiders and the uninitiated may think of Schweitzer as an intellectual heavyweight (hence a thinker "universally admired"—by fools), insiders know him to have been a purveyor of fatuous bromides. *The awareness on the part of the two philosophers of the misunderstanding by the naive first audience is a part of what is being asserted by the ironic remark.* Contained within that awareness (we may assume) is a recollection on their part that they too once thought of Albert Schweitzer as a great philosopher, and an accompanying sense of the distance they have come, and the path they have had to travel, to arrive at their present true evaluation of his supposed wisdom.

The paradigmatic instance of Socratic irony is his provocative assertion that he is ignorant, that he knows nothing and hence that he has nothing to teach. This disclaimer is counterposed to the inflated claim, made by Gorgias and other traveling teachers, that they know the true nature of justice, virtue, shipbuilding, or anything else their listeners wish to learn, and will, for a fee, impart their wisdom. In his encounters with the sophists, Socrates denies possessing any knowledge whatsoever, but he does represent himself as wishing to learn, in the service of which desire he makes so bold as to ask a few apparently simple questions, merely for clarification.

Socrates as we know him is a character in a literary work of art, not a real person. The author of the work is Plato, and we, as the readers of the dialogue, are the true or real audience. Within the dialogue there are in fact two superficial audiences, not one. The first audience is the sophist—Gorgias, let us suppose—together with those other characters in the dialogue who take Gorgias at face value. The second audience, which conceives itself to be the recipient of an ironic communication from Socrates, consists of the band of Socrates' followers, mostly young and of aristocratic birth, among whom Plato, in his youth, was numbered.

Socrates' followers hear him as saying something like this: "I know nothing of the confusions and superficial opinions that Gorgias purveys. In his eyes, therefore, I am ignorant. What I possess is a true understanding of beauty, justice, virtue, and the good life. Were Gorgias half so wise as he pretends to be, he would fall silent and apprentice himself to me. As proof of the superiority of my understanding, I shall expose the inner contradictions of his opinions by a few apparently innocent questions and he—poor fool—will never realize what a mock I have made of him."

This, or something like it, is what Socrates' disciples hear when he utters a self-deprecatory remark. But though they puff themselves as the true audience for Socrates' communications, as the recipients of the esoteric meaning, they are themselves merely a second apparent audience. The true audience is we who read the dialogue. The true Socratic message is that he indeed has nothing to teach, and hence in that sense is ignorant. Philosophic wisdom cannot be taught, not even by the greatest teacher of all. The bright young men smirking among themselves are only a little better than the less sophisticated followers of Gorgias. By exchanging one master for another, they have lost the very heart of the Socratic message, which is that in the quest for self-knowledge there can be no masters, no authorities.

So the Socratic utterance, "I am ignorant," has three levels of meaning, *each a deepening of the one preceding and each reached only through a critique of the one before.* Socrates' wisdom is not a substitute for the self-deceiving opinions of a Gorgias, or for the smug self-congratulation of his own followers. It is a complex whole that *includes* an awareness of those other, more superficial levels. The self-deceit and false wisdom of the sophist and of his pupils are inseparable from the level of rational self-knowledge Socrates has achieved. To give voice to that self-knowledge, he must employ a mode of utterance complex enough to express all the levels or stages through which he has passed, as well as the terminus he has reached. A part of Socrates will always wish to strut and pose, as Gorgias does. Another part longs to be the teacher his disciples believe him to be, the oracle, the fount of wisdom effortlessly transmitted. And yet another part—the truest part, the *real* Socrates—resignedly recognizes and accepts the folly of both wishes. All this is encapsulated within the offhandedly ironic disclaimer, "I am ignorant."

It is obvious to even the casual reader that Plato's use of ironic discourse is dramatically effective. The *Dialogues* are perhaps the most beautiful and powerful philosophy ever written. But Plato accomplishes something more, by his use of irony, than mere drama or literary embellishment. I wish to argue, though I am not certain how I could establish so powerful a claim, that what Plato has to say, in all its complexity and richness, can *only* be said by means of ironic discourse.

Eventually, I shall want to argue that Marx's complex vision of the reality and mystifying appearance of capitalist society can be rendered literarily only by the ironic discourse that we in fact find in *Capital*. First, however, I must say something a good deal more precise about the ontological ground of the sort of irony we encounter in the Platonic *Dialogues*.

It has become a commonplace in recent philosophical discussions that language has many functions beyond that of the assertion of propositions, among them the asking of questions, the giving of orders, and the expressing of feelings or attitudes. It is perhaps less obvious that the complexities of the mind—the interrelationships among conscious and unconscious thoughts and feelings, the ambivalences and ambiguities, the projections, introjections, displacements, and transferences that are the mind's characteristic modes of operation—impose a corresponding complexity on our uses of language.

If it were always the case that I either believe a proposition or do not, have an attitude toward some matter or do not, intend to issue a command or do not, then simple declarative, expressive, or imperative language would suffice for the accurate rendering of thought into language. But what if the reality is more complex than that? For example, what if I can, in some sense, both believe a proposition and not believe it, all at the same time? Indeed, what if there can be one part of me that believes it, and another part that does not, the part of me that does not believe having won the upper hand after an internal struggle? If I wish to give expression fully to this complex situation, what linguistic resources do I require?

To begin with, I must find a way to speak in the voice of that part of me that has won out, and does not believe the proposition, in order to convey the fact that it *has* won out—for in the struggles of the mind it is control of the authorial voice, the "I think" of the unity of apperception, that is the prize. As Kant tells us, the "I think" can be attached to all my representations. It is the implicit frame of all knowledge claims, and the identity of the I who asserts the proposition is an ineradicable part of what is being asserted.

Speaking in that voice, I must say that I do not believe the proposition, while at the same time saying that a part of me does believe it, a part that once controlled the speaking voice but no longer does, a part, however, that is *still a part of me.* And all this must be said in such a way as to convey what it is to assert a proposition *against* the resistance of a part of me, so that my asserting of the proposition is not confused, for example, with the placid, unstressful asserting by one for whom the contrary proposition never had any significant valence. If I were to say, for example, in a neutral, impersonal voice, "A part of me believes such and such, but the real me does not," then I would, by this locution, distance myself so completely from the part of me that still believes as implicitly to deny that it ever had been a part of me at all. Rather, I must convey the fact that I arrived at my disbelief through a criticism of my earlier belief, and that the belief lives on in me, defeated but not obliterated or extruded.

Imagine, for example, that I have been raised in the Catholic faith, and have arrived at my present atheistical condition through a lengthy and painful process of questioning and self-criticism. The symbols, the myths, the liturgy, the language of Catholicism retain for me, as for many lapsed Catholics, a residual power that I cannot wholly subdue, and whose direct and indirect effects in part define who and how I am. If I am asked, "Do you believe in God?" how can I answer in such a way as to communicate this complex state of affairs, with the weights and resonances of the several portions of my religious condition given their proper magnitude?

Simply to answer, "No, I do not" would be, strictly speaking, to lie. It would be to lie by omission, but to lie nonetheless. Such an answer in no way distinguishes me from one who has had no religious upbringing and who has never believed. To say, "I once did, but I no longer do" comes closer, but still misrepresents the true situation by treating the remnants of Catholicism as no longer present *in me*, as having been externalized and destroyed.

We might think that a true, though tedious, answer to the question would be a thorough unpacking of the situation in flat, declarative prose, more or less as I have been doing in these past few paragraphs. But that really will not do. To speak that way is to invent a voice that is *neither* the voice of the victorious portion of myself, *nor* the voice of the subdued portion, but is the voice of an external observer, a scientific reporter, a neutral party not implicated either in the original Catholic faith nor in its rejection. It is the voice of the cultural anthropologist describing native customs, of the social theorist denying complicity in the popular culture of his own society by his very manner of reporting it. Insofar as I purport to be voicing *my* religious condition in *that* voice, I am lying. In all likelihood, I would be deceiving myself at least as much as my audience. What is more, the declarative unpacking of the complexities of my loss of faith would entirely miss the sensuous immediacy of feeling that is an essential part of my present rejection of, and residual clinging to, Catholicism.

Consider now what might be accomplished by means of the adoption of an ironic voice. Asked whether I believe in God, I might reply—employing, ever so faintly exaggeratedly, the singsong tone of the Apostle's Creed—"I believe in God the Father Almighty Creator of Heaven and Earth and in Jesus Christ . . ." These few words, uttered thus, would capture, for an audience capable of understanding what I was saying, the entire state of affairs: that I once was an unreflective communicant of the Roman Catholic faith, that I no longer am, that I view my former beliefs with amusement, rather than with superstitious fear, but that those beliefs, and the associated rituals, still have some power for me, so that what I now am and believe can only be understood as a development out of that earlier, credulous state. To a naive audience, it would of course appear that I was simply answering the question in the affirmative.

Since this point is, in fact, the pivot on which my entire argument turns, I shall belabor it a bit at the risk of growing tiresome. The literary complexity of an ironic reply to the question, "Do you believe in God?" is required by the complexity of the speaking subject who gives the reply. If the self were substantively simple, so that either it believed or did not, asserted or did not, and so on, then simple declarative discourse would suffice. Even if this simple self had emerged from a complex process of development, in the course of which first one belief, then another, first one passion, then another, had held sway, even then, so long as the product of the developmental process were simple, unambiguous discourse would suffice to express its present state. The complexity of the historical development of the self would require no special complexity of expression, so long as that complexity were fully represented in the unified nature of the present ego. But if the speaking self is complex, many-layered, capable of reflection, self-deception, ambivalence, of unconscious thought processes, of projections, introjections, displacements, transferences, and all manner of ambiguities—in short, if the *history* of the self is directly present as part of its current nature—then only a language containing within itself the literary resources corresponding to these complexities will suffice to speak the truth.

In the example we have been discussing, the immediately experienced tension between the antireligious conviction to which I have won my way by an inner struggle and the old, defeated but not banished faith that still asserts its claim upon my allegiance is a part of what I actually believe. It is false to suggest that I *believe* the proposition "There is no God" neutrally, unambivalently, purely assertorically, but also that, as an added and separable fact of my consciousness, I am experiencing certain inner feelings that can be characterized, phenomenologically, as feelings of tension or conflict. The tension is a tension *in* the belief, in such a manner that my belief differs in its nature from that of a complacent atheist who has never known God. It would be strictly false to say that we two believe the same proposition, and it would be manifestly obvious that we might fail to communicate with one another if each of us were to say to the other, in turn, "I do not believe in God."

The Socratic distinction between appearance and reality has been called into question on the grounds that it presupposes an "essentialist" ontology. To call the straightness of the stick the *reality* and my perception of it as bent an *appearance* is to presuppose that there is an objective ground for the claim that the straightness is an essential property of the stick and the bentness a mere subjective mode in which that essential property manifests itself. The same ontological presupposition, it has been argued, is implicit in the theses that profit, rent, and interest are *appearances* of surplus value, that cultural and political institutions are *appearances* of, or manifestations of, the underlying social relationships of production, and that the inner essence of history is class struggle. Such ontological claims, it is said, make philosophical sense *only* on the fundamentally religious premise that being is the product of a purposeful creation, inherent in which is the *telos* of the Creator. Without such a premise, there is no ground for calling one aspect or element of the world *truly real,* and another aspect or element *merely appearance.* Marx, the anti-essentialists observe, frequently speaks in this essentialist way, but he thereby merely manifests the influence of his Hegelian education. They conclude that insofar as we wish to follow Marx in the establishment and development of a scientific theory of society and history, we must put behind us these last philosophical echoes of religious mythology, and develop a theory of capitalism in which the distinction between essence and appearance plays no role.

I embrace this critique of essentialism in the terms in which it is enunciated. I am quite unprepared to readmit into social theory the religious superstitions that were, with such great effort, driven out of philosophy. Nevertheless, I propose to build my entire interpretation of *Capital* on the objectively grounded distinction between appearance and reality. Clearly, a good deal will have to be said to justify such an undertaking.

The preponderance of my argument must wait until my second and third lectures, but I can lay the groundwork for my later discussion by drawing out a significant implication of ironic discourse. In defining irony, I referred to the "real" audience and the "apparent" audience. There are two features of ironic discourse that justify this way of speaking. First, of course, we have access in ironic discourse to the intentions of the speaker. Discourse creates a world that is purposive in its objective nature, since it is the product of intentional acts. But this is, by itself, not enough to justify the locutions "real audience" and "apparent audience," for the speaker's intentions might be frustrated, or indeed might be inherently unfulfillable. The truly crucial feature of ironic discourse that justifies the appearance/reality distinction is the asymmetrical relation between the two meanings of the utterance and the two audiences that receive it.

Irony is not ambiguity. The second, or real, audience hears both meanings and knows that there is a first audience that hears only the first meaning. What is more, the second audience's knowledge of the double meaning, and its awareness of its privileged position vis-à-vis the first audience, *is a part of what it understands when it hears the utterance.* Thus, the real audience's understanding does not merely replace that of the first audience, it incorporates it and transcends it. From an analysis of the first audience's understanding alone, we could never reconstruct the entire situation of ironic communication. But from the understanding of the second audience alone, we could. Thus, the second audience's understanding can legitimately be called epistemologically higher, or superior, and an account of the communicative situation from the standpoint of the second audience can be considered objectively more correct. Furthermore, from an historical or developmental standpoint, the understanding of the second audience can only be a later stage than the understanding of the first audience, for leaving to one side collective amnesia, a movement from the understanding of the second audience to that of the first would represent not merely a *change* in "point of view," but an unambiguous *loss* of knowledge and insight. No one could *first* learn that the stick is straight but looks bent because of the difference in the refractive indices of water and air, and *then* move by a process of education, cultural development, or scientific evolution to the unreflective belief that the stick is, as it appears to be, bent.

Irony is a mode of discourse, hence it is the product of an intentional act. Nature is *not* a mode of discourse, nor is it—setting to one side the illusions of religion—the product of an intentional act. But *society* occupies something of an intermediate status. Society is not the product of a single conscious, purposeful agent—not God, not History, not Objective Spirit, not even Man—but it *is* the collective product of countless purposeful men and women in their complex interractions with one another. If we can successfully defend the claim that the political economy of capitalism has an irreducible element of collective communication, and if we can demonstrate that that communication has something very like an ironic structure, then we may find that we have sound objective grounds for deploying an appearance/reality distinction *without* the philosophically objectionable essentialism of religion or religious philosophy.

The time has come to cease our beating about the neighboring fields, and to confront directly the text and the teaching of Karl Marx. In the central doctrines of *Capital,* as they find expression in Marx's highly dramatic language, we shall find the secret to the ironic structure of the crazy, inverted world of capitalism.

Two

The Factory and the Cave:
The Inverted World of Capitalism

The key to an understanding of *Capital* is the concept of *mystification,* a concept that had played a major role in continental thought of the late eighteenth and early nineteenth centuries, but before Marx, had never systematically been applied to the field of political economy.

It was a commonplace with Marx and Engels, so often repeated as to become a cliché, that the Germans were essentially philosophical (which was to say, religious), the French political, and the English practical (or economic). The first of these three great realms of thought and practice—the philosophical or religious—had been dramatically demystified by Kant's refutations of the claims of rational theology, by David Strauss's assault on the historicity of the Gospels in his influential *Life of Jesus,* and above all by Ludwig Feuerbach's thoroughgoing secularization of God in *The Essence of Christianity.* The effect, Wizard-of-Oz-like, had been to blow away the clouds of incense, revealing the church in its true nature as a secular institution, created by man as an instrument of domination.

The second realm, the political, had been washed clean of *its* especial and peculiar mystery by the bloodbath of the French Revolution. When the head of Europe's most glorious king fell into a basket and the heavens did not open, the aura of monarchy was forever dissipated. There were attempts, of course, to revive the corpse, most notably Hegel's desperate defense of the majesty of the ruler. Indeed, one of Marx's most serious early efforts at philosophical criticism is aimed at that defense. *A Contribution to the Critique of Hegel's Philosophy of Right,* despite its almost impenetrable obscurity, is a shrewd and focused attack on the first premise of the mystified state, namely the claim that the existence of the state is logically and ontologically prior to that of its subjects, and hence that the state takes moral and political precedence over them as well.

Needless to say, new mystifications of the state were readied to replace the old. As the divine right of kings retreated to the nursery, there to take up residence in fairy tales of peasant maids and frog princes, the doctrine of popular sovereignty stepped forward as the new sophistry by which power misrepresented itself as authority. With the hindsight of yet another century, we are forced to acknowledge the tenacity of these myths of the state. As the churches empty, the public squares fill up with deluded citizens ready to cheer the latest pretender to state authority.

In his youth, Marx was much concerned with the mystifications of church and state. However, when he turned to the third great realm—the economic—he encountered a special problem, reminiscent of that with which Socrates had wrestled. For the economy did not seem to call for demystification. Mysteries there might be in the throne room or the sacristy, but what mysteries could lurk in the marketplace? There all was plain as day. Men came to trade, to bargain, to advance their individual interest as shrewdly as they might. They wore everyday clothes, not ritual garments tricked out

with precious gems in iconic patterns. They spoke the de-
motic tongue, priding themselves on being simple, straightforward, no-nonsense men.

The political economists who recorded and anatomized the
doings of the marketplace reflected this simplicity, this absence of pendulous transcendent significance, of shadow and
echo. Adam Smith and David Ricardo, James Mill and
Jeremy Bentham, John Stuart Mill, all wrote a transparent,
serviceable prose—clear, efficient, devoid of the metaphor
and metaphysics that clouded the great rationalizations of
church and state. Land, labor, and capital. Equals exchanged
for equals in a sunlit market where every interaction was a
contract, every contract a quid pro quo and the law enforced
all contracts with blind impartiality. The English had no head
for theological subtleties, and *their* Reformation, unlike Germany's, had arisen more from the concerns of the flesh than
from those of the spirit. Their brutal truncation of monarchy
had been softened by the compromises of the Glorious Revolution. Where better than in England to observe the plain
dealings of the market, free of the lingering wisps of religion
or monarchy?

Or so it seemed. For Marx was persuaded that the market
was more deeply mystified than ever the altar or the throne
had been. The market was a strange and ghostly place, inhab-
ited by things that behaved like people, and people who were
treated, and came to treat themselves, as things.

Marx's predecessors had failed to discern any mystery in
the exchange of commodities on the market. There were
puzzles, to be sure; theoretical problems, such as the nature
of rent, or the consequences of taxation; but not *mysteries.*
The market, they supposed, was a realm of scientific investigation from which the last ghostly shreds of mystification

had been blown away by the clean air of secular reason. But Marx thought that the "scientific" explanations of the classical economists, apparently so straightforward and empirical, were in fact wildly metaphysical.

Why then take up the language and concepts of so unsatisfactory a theory? Why not simply brush the theory aside and put in its place a new and better account of capitalism? Or, at the very least, why not quickly and effectively expose the mystifications to an audience already attuned to the secular?

Alas, demystification presupposes the acknowledgement of mystery, and the classical political economists were unaware of any mystery in the marketplace. The communicant, in the presence of the Host, experiences a tremulous awe that cries out to the secular mind to be explained—or explained away. But the political economist, confronted by a commodity, feels no tingle of divinity, no sense of things unsaid and unseen. Marx's first problem is thus like Socrates': He must lead his audience to the recognition that they are in need of enlightenment before he can even begin to provide it.

Marx undertakes, in a theoretical tour de force, to extract his own doctrine of exploitation and accumulation from the bowels of classical political economy by demonstrating that the Ricardian theory of value is incapable of accounting for the central phenomenon of capitalism, namely profit. He must therefore begin with the mystified premises of value theory in order simultaneously to expose and transcend them.

More subtly, Marx wishes to assert, as an indispensable tenet of his analysis of capitalism, that the particular obfuscations exhibited in classical political economy are the necessary and characteristic mode in which capitalist social relations *misrepresent* themselves. Every mode of production, he argues, rationalizes its social relationships of production in a distinctive manner. Capitalism's strategy of justification is to present a surface appearance of justice and equal exchange, so concealing its fundamental exploitative nature as to appear to have nothing to hide.

Marx must find a language that will permit him to do three things at once. His language must express the mysteriousness of our daily experience of commodity production and exchange; it must lead us to confront that mysteriousness; and it must help us to dispel the illusion so that we may apprehend the real nature of capitalist social relations and move beyond the false clarity of classical political economy to a true understanding of exploitation, accumulation, and crisis.

Marx seeks, furthermore, a discourse that will permit him, while accomplishing this complex effort of demystification, still to capture and express the extent to which he, and we, as participants in the mystified social order of capitalism, preserve its illusions, fetishisms, and mysteries even as we expose them and strive to overcome them. We shall find that Marx's language in the opening chapters of *Capital* is artfully devised for these purposes, while permitting the expression of complex moral sentiments in a fashion that would be prohibited by the style of *Value, Price, and Profit.* Indeed, it is not too strong to say that *Capital* is a work of high literary art whose dominant metaphors, ironic structure, and authorial voice subserve a deliberate philosophical purpose.

Now, as Portnoy's psychiatrist says, let us begin.

The wealth of societies in which the capitalist mode of production prevails, appears as an "immense collection of commodities," the individual commodity as its elementary form. Our investigation begins, therefore, with the analysis of the commodity.[1]

The principal verb of the opening sentence of *Capital* is *erscheinen als,* "appears as." Marx chooses to begin his analysis of capitalism, and of the theories of capitalism advanced by his predecessors, at the level of appearances, thereby invoking the distinction between appearance and reality on which his entire theoretical enterprise depends.

The image conjured by Marx is a striking one. We begin with the marketplace, the sphere of circulation, where what we first encounter as we look about us is enormous heaps of consumer goods. At the most superficial level, capitalism is a cornucopia from which tumble in great profusion coats, shoes, carriages, loaves of bread, and bottles of wine. We can compare Marx's figure with Engels's vivid description in the third chapter of *The Condition of the Working Class in England* of the city of Manchester, as it had grown during the Industrial Revolution. Manchester, Engels tells us, is a sort of architectural embodiment of the contrast between appearance and reality:

> The town itself is peculiarly built, so that a person may live in it for years, and go in and out daily without coming into contact with a working-people's quarter or even with workers, that is, so long as he confines himself to his business or to pleasure walks. . . . Manchester contains, at its heart, a rather extended commercial district, perhaps half a mile long and about as broad, and consisting

1   Karl Marx, *Capital: A Critique of Political Economy,* vol. 1, trans. (from the 3d German edition) Samuel Moore and Edward Aveling (New York: International Publishers, 1967), 35. Subsequent references to volume 1 are indicated by parenthetical pagination in the text.

almost wholly of offices and warehouses. . . . The members of [the] money aristocracy can take the shortest road through the middle of all the labouring districts to their places of business without ever seeing that they are in the midst of the grimy misery that lurks to the right and the left. For the thoroughfares leading from the Exchange in all directions out of the city are lined, on both sides, with an almost unbroken series of shops.[2]

"A commodity" Marx says, "is, in the first place, an object outside us, a thing that by its properties satisfies human wants of some sort or another" (35). The properties of a commodity in virtue of which it satisfies human wants are aspects of it as a natural object—its weight, color, texture, potentiality for chemical interactions, and so forth. The commodity, qua natural object, possesses these properties wherever and whenever it exists. Magically remove a loaf of bread ten thousand miles or ten thousand years from the place where it has been baked and it will nourish as well. A coat will protect us from the elements under any social, historical, or ideological conditions. Hence it would *appear*, if we are hardheaded, sensible empiricists, that the natural properties of commodities are its *real* properties, and anything science can tell us about these real properties will serve to reveal their essential nature to us. In fact, however, this inference is merely the first of a series of misleading and mystifying inversions by which, in the realm of the economic, reality is made to change places with appearance. Further investigation reveals that commodities, strictly speaking, are not physical objects at all. The natural properties of commodities, the

2   Friedrich Engels, *The Condition of the Working Class in England,* in *Karl Marx/Friedrich Engels Collected Works,* vol. 4 (New York: International Publishers, 1975), 347–48.

properties that first strike our senses as we windowshop along the shop-lined avenues of Manchester, are *strictly speaking* not properties of commodities at all. For, as Marx himself tells us, a commodity "is, in reality, a very queer thing, abounding in metaphysical subtleties and theological niceties" (71).

Indeed, a commodity, *strictly speaking,* is not an object of sense perception at all. Ten yards of linen, qua cloth, can be seen, felt, cut, sewn, folded, packaged, and transported from a factory to a retail outlet. But ten yards of linen, qua commodity, cannot be seen, felt, or physically manipulated. For a commodity is a queer thing, a thing full of metaphysical subtleties and theological niceties. Only the doubting Thomases of this world sniff the sacramental wine as the chalice is passed to them, expecting somehow that through the miracle of transubstantiation the sweet odor of wine will give way to the stench of blood.

But if commodities are not physical objects, what then are they? Or, to put the same question somewhat differently, *in virtue of what* are the linen, the coat, the corn, and the iron commodities? Here is Marx's answer, which I shall quote at some length.

> If then we leave out of consideration the use-value of commodities, they have only one common property left, that of being products of labour. But even the product of labour itself has undergone a change in our hands. If we make abstraction from its use-value, we make abstraction at the same time from the material elements and shapes that make the product a use-value; we see in it no longer a table, a house, yarn, or any other useful thing. Its existence as a material thing is put out of sight. Neither can it any longer be regarded as the product of the labour

of the joiner, the mason, the spinner, or of any other definite kind of productive labour. Along with the useful qualities of the products themselves, we put out of sight both the useful character of the various kinds of labour embodied in them, and the concrete forms of that labour; there is nothing left but what is common to them all; all are reduced to one and the same sort of labour, human labour in the abstract.

Let us now consider the residue of each of these products. It consists of the same unsubstantial reality in each, a mere congelation of homogeneous human labour, of labour-power expended without regard to the mode of its expenditure. All that these things now tell us is, that human labour-power has been expended in their production, that human labour is embodied in them. As crystals of this social substance, common to them all, they are values—commodity values. . . . The labour, however, that forms the substance of value, is homogeneous labour, expenditure of one uniform labour-power. (38–39)

The exchange value of a commodity—or, more precisely, the exchange value in virtue of which a commodity *is* a commodity, the exchange value that constitutes the commodityness of a commodity—is a *crystal of abstract homogeneous social labor*. The quantum of exchange value congealed or crystallized in each commodity can neither be seen nor felt nor smelt nor tasted. This homogeneous, infinitely divisible, nonsensory stuff, this *value*, is contained in the products of labor as a consequence of their being produced by workers hired by capitalists in a system of market exchange regulated by competition. In the production process, portions of this stuff congealed in previously produced commodities are transmitted or passed on to newly produced commodities. As the spindle turns, it smoothly, invisibly, magically passes on infinitesimal bits of its value to the thread that collects around it. When the spindle breaks and must be discarded, it is emptied of its crystals of value, exhausted, spent—unless of course, it has yet some resale value as a used spindle, in which case it will be found to have held back a little cache of its secret value to bring, as a dowry, to its new owner.

The passionate aim and single-minded purpose of the hardheaded businessmen from Manchester and Liverpool, London and Sheffield, are to accumulate as much of this transcendent ectoplasmic stuff as possible, as fast as possible. They want it, not for its attractive and gratifying sensory qualities—for it has no sensory qualities at all—but for its magical ability to increase in quantity. They want it, that is to say, so that they may get more of it, which they want in order to get still more. When they grow old and rich, these metaphysical entrepreneurs may decline into sensation, and cash in their crystals of value for inferior things of the flesh, for houses and clothes and rare paintings. But so long as they are young and vigorous, they shun all such temptations and pursue the holy grail of self-expanding value.

What can Marx possibly have in mind by advancing so manifestly absurd an account of the commodity? That he *does* consider this theory of "crystals of abstract homogeneous socially necessary labor" to be absurd is demonstrated by the language in which he chooses to expound it. The chapter on commodities, in which this extraordinary doctrine is introduced, is strewn with religious metaphors. Marx sets himself to trace the "genesis" of the money form of exchange value. As coats and linen change and exchange in a ghostly minuet, the linen, he says, "acquires a value-form different from its physical form," an echo of the miracle of transubstantiation. (Indeed, all exchange is a kind of inverted transubstantiation, for in the miracle of the mass, the sensory accidents of the bread and wine remain unaltered, while their essence or substance is changed into that of the body and blood of Christ, whereas in commodity exchange, while the sensory accidents of one commodity are exchanged for the sensory accidents of another, their substance—value— remains unaltered.) "The fact that [the linen] is value," Marx observes, "is made manifest by its equality with the coat, just as the sheep-like nature of a Christian is shown in his resemblance to the Lamb of God" (52).

Lest there be any reader so insensitive to even the broadest mockery as to imagine that this account of the inner essence of commodities is meant literally as a straightforward description of what makes anything a commodity, Marx breaks the ironic tone of his discourse momentarily, near the end of the chapter, to tell us that such talk is deranged, crack-brained, crazy—*verrückt:*

> If I state that coats and boots stand in relation to linen, because it is the universal incarnation of human labour, the craziness [*die Verrücktheit*] of the statement is self-evident. Nevertheless, if the producers of coats and boots compare those articles with linen, or, what is the same thing, with gold and silver, as the universal equivalent, they express the relation between their own private labour, and the collective labour of society in the same deranged form. (76)

It will require the remainder of this lecture, and all of the following lecture, to clarify Marx's complex reasons for defining the commodity in this deliberately crack-brained way. The full explanation, as we shall see, requires a thorough explication of the ontological and social status of money, and of the dynamics of economic crises, tasks to which my talents would, alas, be inadequate even with a world of time. Nevertheless, we *can* make a start, and the first step must be an exploration, in Marx's writings, of the theme of *inversion*.

The notions of inversion and of the inverted world are introduced by Hegel in his discussion of understanding (in the Kantian sense of the cognitive faculty that orders the given materials of experience in lawlike structures) and of the relationship between appearance and that which appears. Hegel's account of these notions, like so much of his philosophy, is exceedingly obscure, but the central theme is a rejection of Kant's claim that the perceived world, the world of scientific investigation and daily experience, is merely an appearance of a real world of things as they are in themselves, lying behind the presented appearances. In effect, what happens is something like this: We begin *in medias res* with a multiplicity of events and objects in relation to one another, and by a process of abstraction and cognitive organization we posit a system of laws as the order, or form, or structure of the experienced world. This "world" of laws is "supersensible" in the sense that it is posited by the mind's own cognitive powers, not apprehended in sense-experience. It is a world characterized by universality rather than by particularity, for the events and objects with which we begin are individual, local, occurring at a specific time and in a specific place, whereas the laws of the "supersensible" world are universal, general, applicable to all times and all places. Furthermore, the supersensible world is characterized by necessity rather than by contingency, for the laws of nature are conceived as laws of necessary connection, causal laws, whereas the concatenation of events in the world of sense-experience is experienced merely as given, as happening without necessity.

Now, however, by an inversion, this supersensible world of laws is construed as the *real* world of which the realm of particular events and objects is only an instantiation, an unfolding, an embodiment. What was ectype is now construed as archetype. As Hegel says:

> By means of this principle, the first supersensible world, the changeless kingdom of laws, the immediate ectype and copy of the world of perception, has turned round into its opposite. . . . This second supersensible world is in this way the inverted world, and, moreover, since one aspect is already present in the first supersensible world, the inverted form of the first.[3]

The Hegelian notion of inversion crops up repeatedly in Marx's mature thought. Money, which is originally a medium for expressing the value of commodities, comes, by an inversion, to be construed as value itself, so that costly commodities are thought of as valuable *because* they are expensive. At first, goods are produced for the purpose of satisfying human needs, and exchanged only when there is a bit left over after those needs have been satisfied. Eventually, goods come to be produced for the purpose of being exchanged, and their capacity to satisfy needs is seen simply as a means to that end. The human capacity for productive work is, by a parallel inversion, transformed from an end in itself to a mere means to other ends, so that the fulfilled human being who lives to work is replaced by the diminished and alienated laborer who works to live.

Indeed, the broad literary structure of *Capital* as a whole can best be understood as a dramatic inversion. It is a com-

3   G. W. F. Hegel, *The Phenomenology of Mind,* trans. (with an introduction and notes) J. B. Baillie (London: Swan Sonnenschein and Co., Ltd., 1910), 151–52.

monplace that Marx was a materialist, that he conceived himself as having inverted Hegel. As Marx says in the famous afterword to the second edition of volume one of *Capital:*

> I openly avowed myself the pupil of that mighty thinker, and even here and there, in the chapter on value, coquetted with the modes of expression peculiar to him. The mystification which dialectic suffers in Hegel's hands, by no means prevents him from being the first to present its general form of working in a comprehensive and conscious manner. With him it is standing on its head. It must be turned right side up again, if you would discover the rational kernel within the mystical shell. (19–20)

But the greatest metaphor of idealist philosophy is to be found not in the writings of Hegel but in the *Republic* of Plato, in one of the best-known passages of ancient philosophy, the Allegory of the Cave.

Plato compares the human condition to that of men and women chained to the floor of a deep cave, on whose wall appear the shadows of objects carried before flickering fires. In this subterranean realm of appearances, the captives ignorantly strive to guess the order in which the images will pass before their eyes, neither knowing nor caring that what they see are but copies or reflections, dimly lit by the merest sparks of the divine fire. One brave soul frees himself from his bonds and struggles to the surface, where, bursting forth into the sunlight, he apprehends reality and comes thereby to recognize the phenomenal character of the realm he has left. That image, of the darkened cave below and the bright open spaces above, has come down to us across two thousand years as the controlling metaphor of appearance and reality.

In *Capital,* Marx dramatically reverses the metaphor, and

by so doing declares his liberation from the mystifications of idealism. For Marx, the sunlit marketplace, the very Eden, as he so bitterly describes it, of the rights of man, the natural home of Freedom, Equality, Property, and Bentham, is the realm of appearances. Reality lies behind the factory door, within the dimly lighted workrooms, where men, women, and children are chained for endless hours to brutal machines. In the flickering light of *that* cave can be seen the truth of capitalism. The essence of capitalism is profit, and profit is created not in the marketplace, where equals are exchanged for equals, but in the factory. As the laborers stumble out of the door of the factory, they leave behind them for a few hours the reality of capitalism, and fleetingly take on the appearance of citizens of the commonwealth of liberty.

Thus Marx redeems the promise of the opening sentences of *Capital*, in which he signals his intention to dispel the illusions of the market. It is in the production of commodities, not in their exchange, that the secret of capitalism lies. The transformation of labor-power from a human capacity into an alienable commodity—a transformation that rests historically on the separation of the worker from the means of production—gives rise to a system of exchange in which the value of goods appears, or manifests itself, as abstract, homogeneous, socially necessary labor.

I should like, in the time that remains, to explore with you Marx's development of this concept of abstract labor, by way of an odd and striking contrast with a bit of youthful buffoonery from one of his earliest published writings.

In 1844, when Marx was twenty-six, he and Engels cooperated on *The Holy Family*, an enormously bloated, bizarre, uproarious attack on the Bauer brothers, Bruno and Edgar, and their associates, the Young Hegelians. In an attack on

F. Z. Zychlinski's discussion of Eugene Sue's popular novel, *Les Mystères de Paris,* Marx develops a brilliant burlesque of the logic of idealist metaphysics. Here, at some length, is an extract that captures the zany quality of Marx's critique.

> The mystery of the Critical presentation of the *Mystères de Paris* is the mystery of the *speculative, of Hegelian construction.* . . . A few words will suffice to characterise speculative construction *in general.* . . .
>
> If from real apples, pears, strawberries and almonds I form the general idea *"Fruit,"* if I go further and *imagine* that my abstract idea *"Fruit,"* derived from real fruit, is an entity existing outside me, is indeed the *true* essence of the pear, the apple, etc., then—in the *language of speculative* philosophy—I am declaring that *"Fruit"* is the *"Substance"* of the pear, the apple, the almond, etc. I am saying, therefore, that to be a pear is not essential to the pear, that to be an apple is not essential to the apple; that what is essential to these things is not their real existence, perceptible to the senses, but the essence that I have abstracted from them and then foisted on them, the essence of my idea—*"Fruit."* I therefore declare apples, pears, almonds, etc., to be mere forms of existence, *modi,* of *"Fruit."* . . . Having reduced the different real fruits to the *one* "fruit" of abstraction—*"the* Fruit," speculation must, in order to attain some semblance of real content, try somehow to find its way back from *"the* Fruit," from the *Substance* to the *diverse,* ordinary real fruits, the pear, the apple, the almond, etc. . . . If apples, pears, almonds and strawberries are really nothing but *"the* Substance," *"the* Fruit," the question arises: Why does *"the* Fruit" manifest itself to me sometimes as an apple, sometimes as a pear, sometimes as an almond?

Why this *semblance of diversity* which so obviously con-
tradicts my speculative conception of *Unity*, "*the* Substance," "*the* Fruit"?

This, answers the speculative philosopher, is because
"*the* Fruit" is not dead, undifferentiated, motionless, but
a living, self-differentiating, moving essence. . . . The different profane fruits are different manifestations of the
life of the "*one* Fruit"; they are crystallisations of "*the*
Fruit" itself. . . . We see that if the Christian religion
knows only *one* Incarnation of God, speculative philosophy has as many incarnations as there are things, just as
it has here in every fruit an incarnation of the Substance,
of the Absolute Fruit.[4]

This comic disquisition on the Absolute Fruit takes on a
richer significance when it is compared with his treatment of
abstract labor in the first chapter of *Capital*. Let us recall that
Marx accorded to his account of abstract labor pride of place
as one of the most important ideas in his great work: "The
best things in my book" (he says in the 24 August 1867 letter
to Engels) "are: 1. (on this depends *all* understanding of the
facts) the *double nature of labour*, according as it is expressed in use-value or exchange value—which even in the
first chapter is prominently displayed."[5] A close look at the
text shows that Marx, with all seriousness, develops the concept of abstract homogeneous socially necessary labor in a
manner parallel to the satirical exposition of the concept of
the Absolute Fruit. When we have grasped the inner significance of this odd convergence, we shall be a good deal closer
to a satisfactory understanding of Marx's conception of the
crazy structure of social reality.

4 *Marx/Engels: Collected Works*, 4:57–59.
5 *Marx-Engels Werke*, B. 31, S. 326.

The development of the concept of abstract labor begins in the opening section of chapter one. We start with concrete particular physical objects whose natural properties make them capable of satisfying various human wants, and whose existence results from particular concrete acts of human laboring—specific acts of weaving, sewing, spinning, and so forth. We "make abstraction from" or "put out of sight" both "the useful character of the various forms of labour" embodied in those physical objects, and also "the concrete forms of that labour." What is left when we have completed this process of abstraction is merely "what is common to them all," namely "human labour in the abstract" (38).

Thus far, we are describing a familiar process of intellectual or conceptual abstraction, of the sort that is required to bring many particular concrete instances under one general heading. Now, however, a series of quite complex conceptual and theoretical shifts take place.

According to Marx, when commodities exchange, "their exchange-value manifests itself as something totally independent of their use-value" (38), from which he draws the conclusion that "the common substance that manifests itself in the exchange-value of commodities, whenever they are exchanged, is their value." And a useful article *has* value, according to Marx, "only because human labour in the abstract has been embodied or materialised in it" (38). After setting aside the superficial error of supposing that a commodity less efficiently and hence more laboriously produced will thereby acquire greater value—a natural enough error, so long as we confusedly think of abstract labor as some peculiar sort of human activity engaged in by abstract laborers in an abstract factory—Marx sums up his analysis:

> We see then that that which determines the magnitude
> of the value of any article is the amount of labour socially

necessary, or the labour-time socially necessary for its production. (39)

Echoing the language of *The Holy Family,* Marx says, "In general, the greater the productiveness of labour, the less is the labour-time required for the production of an article, the less is the amount of labour crystallised [*sic*] in that article, and the less is its value" (40).

As the chapter unfolds, a subtle shift takes place. Marx is elaborating on "the two-fold character of the labour embodied in commodities," and he observes that the coat and linen in the simple example he has been pursuing are, insofar as they are values, "things of like substance, objective expressions of essentially identical labour." But tailoring and weaving, taking them as actual concrete human activities, are "different kinds of labour" (43). So if exchange is to be based on the equating of quanta of abstract labor whose concrete instantiations are quite diverse, some sort of process of *real* abstraction must take place.

There is a linguistic oddity in Marx's discussion which, if we subject it to a strenuous construal, is revelatory of a very profound and important conceptual shift. Marx says not that the coat and linen *have* value, but that they *are* values. Now this is a peculiar diction. We might at first be inclined to treat "the coat and the linen are values" simply as elliptical for "the coat and the linen are objects that have value." But that would be a mistake. To say that the coat and the linen, *qua* commodities, *are* values is to say that the coat and the linen, *qua* commodities, are not natural objects at all. Indeed, it signals the possibility that commodities, strictly so-called, are not substantives, save in a quite superficial grammatical sense, and that, in the language of modern logic, "commodity" and its cognates are syncategorematic terms that can be defined only be explicating the contexts in which they characteristically appear. If this is in fact the case, then the question "what is a commodity?" would be grammatically misleading, and the "correct" answer, namely, "a commodity is a crystall-isation of abstract homogeneous socially necessary labour," would be thoroughly metaphysically misleading.

Marx begins the conceptual inversion of particular and universal by suggesting that "tailoring and weaving . . . are each a productive expenditure of human brains, nerves, and muscles, and in this sense are human labour" (44). Thus far he sounds quite matter-of-factly materialistic, although the use of the word "productive" should serve as a warning, since what counts as *productive* in a competitive capitalist econ-omy is a function of equilibrium prices and profit rates, not of human nerves and muscles. Now, however, he asserts that the tailoring and weaving "are but two different modes of expending human labour-power" (44). This, I suggest, is an echo of the satirical remark, written twenty years earlier, that "apples, pears, almonds, etc. [are] mere forms of exis-tence, *modi,* of '*Fruit*'." The remark is deliberately absurd when made of apples and almonds. It can hardly be meant to be taken as unambiguously serious when made of tailoring and weaving.

By the time Marx is deep into his exposition of the forms of value, the inversion is far advanced. After a complex passage in which Marx, mocking the classical economists, speaks of the "mystical character of gold and silver" (a clear sign that things are not what they seem), he writes:

> The body of the commodity that serves as the equiv-alent, figures as the materialisation of human labour in the abstract, and is at the same time the product of some specifically useful concrete labour. This concrete labour

becomes, therefore, the medium for expressing abstract human labour. If on the one hand the coat ranks as nothing but the embodiment of abstract human labour, so, on the other hand, the tailoring which is actually embodied in it, counts as nothing but the form under which that abstract labour is realised. In the expression of value of the linen, the utility of the tailoring consists, not in making clothes, but in making an object, which we at once recognise to be Value, and therefore to be a congelation of labour, but of labour indistinguishable from that realised in the value of the linen. In order to act as such a mirror of value, the labour of tailoring must reflect nothing but its own abstract quality of being human labour generally. (58)

Tailoring and weaving are human activities. Abstract homogeneous socially necessary labor is an abstraction derived *from* tailoring and weaving by "leaving out of consideration" the myriad particular ways in which they differ from one another. Abstract labor has no existence outside our minds, any more than the fruit has an existence outside our activity of abstracting from the particularities of apples, pears, and almonds. But now an inversion has begun to take place. Hedging slightly, Marx says, "If on the one hand the coat ranks as nothing but the embodiment of abstract human labour . . . ," thereby leaving open the possibility that it is merely *we* who so construe it. But the assertion is made flatly a few pages further on. "The manifold concrete useful kinds of labour, embodied in these different commodities, rank now as so many different forms of the realisation, or manifestation of undifferentiated human labour" (64). What is this but a direct echo of the crack-brained notion, attributed in *The Holy Family* to "the speculative philosopher," that "the different ordinary fruits are different manifestations of the life of the "*one* Fruit"!

Finally, in the section oddly entitled "The Fetishism of Commodities and the Secret Thereof," Marx tells us flat out that this way of speaking and thinking is crazy. "When I state that coats or boots stand in a relation to linen, because it is the universal incarnation of abstract human labour, the craziness [*die Verrücktheit*] of the statement is self-evident. Nevertheless, when the producers of coats and boots compare those articles with linen, or *what is the same thing* [my emphasis], with gold and silver, as the universal equivalent, they express the relation between their own private labour and the collective labour of society in the same crazy form" (76).

So, to speak of tailoring and weaving as manifestations of, embodiments of, forms of the realization of abstract human labor is as crazy, as manifestly inverted, as to speak of man as having been made in God's image, or of apples and pears as different manifestations of the life of the Absolute Fruit. And yet, having alerted us to this absurdity, having burlesqued it in his youth and anatomized it in his maturity, Marx persists in speaking this way throughout *Capital*. Why?

Three

Mrs. Feinschmeck's Blintzes

or

Notes on the Crackpot Categories of Bourgeois Political Economy

Heaven forbid that I should suggest a structural parallel between the first volume of *Capital and Portnoy's Complaint!* Nevertheless, I propose to show you that the famous, and notoriously difficult, analysis of the concept of value in chapter one of *Capital* is in fact an inversion of an old Jewish joke. A bit of borscht-circuit hermeneutics should get us a good deal closer to Marx's central thesis that the categories of bourgeois political economy are fundamentally *verrückt,* crack-brained.

Mrs. Feinschmeck's little boy Reuben developed a terrible phobia about blintzes. Whenever Mrs. Feinschmeck brought a platter of delicious cheese blintzes to the table, Reuben would let out a cry of terror and flee to his room. As blintzes were the pièce de résistance of Mrs. Feinschmeck's culinary repertoire, this posed a serious domestic problem. Mrs. Feinschmeck pleaded and wept. Mr. Feinschmeck threatened and also wept. But nothing could woo Reuben from his irrational fear of blintzes. Finally, in desperation, Mrs. Feinschmeck sought the advice and counsel of the leader of the Reformed Temple, Dr. Lewis (son of Reb Levi, the leader of the Orthodox community). Dr. Lewis, who had studied abnormal psychology and psychiatric counseling at Brandeis University, opined that Reuben's phobia grew out of nothing more than an inadequate understanding of the nature of the blintz. If Mrs. Feinschmeck would take Reuben into the kitchen and proceed step by step before his very eyes through the making of blintzes, Reuben would see that there was nothing mysterious or ominous in the component elements of the blintz. By accustoming himself slowly to the coming-into-being of the blintz, Reuben would lose his phobic fear. For, as the great (albeit goyische) philosopher Immanuel Kant had observed, "Reason has insight only into that which it produces after a plan of its own."

Mrs. Feinschmeck dutifully gathered up the ingredients, sat Reuben on a kitchen chair in full view of the worktable and stove, and began to make blintzes. At each stage, she turned to Reuben to see whether he was becoming frightened. She mixed up the filling. "Is it all right, Reuben?" "It's all right, Mama." She made the batter. "Is it all right, Reuben?" "It's all right, Mama." She made the first paper-thin pancake, laid it on the table, and placed a big spoonful of filling in the middle of the pancake. "Is it all right, Reuben?" "It's all right, Mama,"

She folded over the first corner. "I'm all right, Mama." She folded the second corner. "I'm all right, Mama." She folded the third corner. "I'm still all right, Mama." Finally, she folded over the last corner. "And there it is, Reuben."

"Heeeeeelllllllpppp!!!! BLINTZES!!!!!!"

The joke is, if I may put it this way, an Enlightenment joke. Phobias are superstitions grounded in an inadequate understanding of nature, society, or culture (the blintz being, at one and the same time, a natural object, a social product, and a cultural icon). The appropriate way to dispel a phobia is to offer a rational explication of the origin and structure of its object. The humor of the joke—such as it may be—derives from the fact that Reuben remains atavistically, irrationally afraid of blintzes, even though it has been demonstrated to him with the clarity of a Voltaire that there is nothing frightening, unexpected, or inexplicable in the pancake, the filling, or the fourfold process by which the two are combined.

In chapter one of *Capital,* Marx inverts this joke, thereby calling into question the underlying Enlightenment premise of the rationality of social reality. For twenty-five pages he stirs and cooks his mystified metaphysical categories of value until at the end, with a last turn of the pancake, he presents us with the most commonplace, unmysterious phenomenon of capitalist life—a list of prices. The contrast between the vexatious oddity of the derivation and the banality of the product forces us to recognize that our best-loved, most comforting economic concepts are through and through crazy. For, as Marx reminds us on the very next page, a commodity is a very queer thing, "abounding in metaphysical subtleties and theological niceties" (71).

The story begins (for it is, in its way, the longest shaggy dog story in the annals of political economy) with the opening paragraph of the third section of chapter one:

Commodities come into the world in the shape of use-values, articles, or goods, such as iron, linen, corn, etc. This is their plain, homely, bodily form. They are, however, commodities, only because they are something two-fold, both objects of utility, and, at the same time, depositories of value. They manifest themselves therefore as commodities, or have the form of commodities, only in so far as they have two forms, a physical or natural form and a value-form. (47)

The physical or natural form of commodities, their character as natural objects, poses no philosophical problems, however difficult it may be for science to give us adequate explanations of such properties as magnetism or color. But the *value* of a commodity is another matter.

Turn and examine a single commodity, by itself, as we will [Marx observes], yet in so far as it remains an object of value, it seems impossible to grasp it. (47)

Commodities have a "value-form," as Marx puts it, which contrasts markedly with their natural form. We experience commodities not only as physical objects with the most varied natural properties, but also as *things having value*. Commodities do not merely have price tags attached. They present themselves to us as value incarnate, as entities whose essence is their monetary worth. Marx proposes to trace "the genesis of this money-form," to "develop the expression of value implied in the value-relation of commodities, from its simplest, almost imperceptible outline, to the dazzling money-form" (47–48).

What exactly is the puzzle Marx seeks to solve? Where is the mystery to be dispelled? Ricardo and the classical economists explained money-prices as exchange ratios between a variety of commodities and a particular commodity arbitrarily selected as numeraire. Once we understand the notion of an exchange ratio—understand furthermore, how competition and market exchange bring about a system of stable, regular, consistent exchange ratios—there is nothing more to be explained. Money-prices are merely relative prices, or exchange ratios, expressed in terms of the numeraire.

The classical account of relative price is perfectly correct as an explanation of exchange ratios, and Marx endorses it in the course of his discussion. But it is a grave mistake, he believes, to suppose that there is nothing more to be said. In fact, there is everything more to be said, for the classical account is utterly unable to explain the nature of money, unable consequently to explain the nature and inevitability of economic crises and the instability of capitalism. The classical account of relative price, by portraying the system of relative prices as a rational representation of stable exchange ratios regulated by labor-costs of production, systematically conceals the inherent contradictions of capitalism and serves as an ideological mask for the craziness of bourgeois society.

Let us begin by reminding ourselves of the way in which we actually perceive commodities, as opposed to the way in which they are spoken of in economics textbooks. All of us, by the time we are old enough to buy candy at the corner store or play an arcade game, have learned to experience the price of a commodity, its cost, its value, as one of its intrinsic properties. A Mercedes-Benz *looks* expensive. We don't need to rehearse its exchange ratios with potatoes or shoes or home computers. We simply see it as expensive, as worth a great deal, just as we see elephants as large or feel lead as heavy. Show me a side chair with carved legs, and I will admire it. Tell me that it is a Goddard piece worth twenty-five thousand dollars and the wood begins to glow. Prove to a collector of fine paintings that her Corot is a fake and it will dwindle in her eyes, not merely in her account book. We speak of fabrics as having a "rich" texture, of furnishings as "reeking of money." The *value* of commodities is as immediately given to us as their colors, tastes, and shapes.

Marx subjects these commonplace beliefs and assumptions to a devastating critique. Like Socrates, he uses our unreflective convictions, our unexamined experiences, as a foil for his revelation of the exploitative foundations of capitalism. The starting point for his critique—and, as we shall see, the essential conceptual mystification—is the experience of commodities as quanta of value. Everything in *Capital* depends upon that starting point.

The experience of commodities as quanta of embodied value is universal in capitalist society. Even we few who have achieved a critical ironic distance from capitalism have the experience countless times in every day. What is more—and this, of course, is at the heart of Marx's argument—we *must* experience commodities in this way to function efficiently in a capitalist world. Those who are truly innocent of the value-form of commodities walk through the world, like Prince Myshkin, as idiots.

As an intellectual tour de force, Marx undertakes to draw the secret of money and the value-form of commodities out of the most elementary value relation imaginable. He begins with what he calls the Elementary or Accidental Form of Value.

> The simplest value-relation is evidently that of one commodity to some one other commodity of a different kind. Hence the relation between the values of two commodities supplies us with the simplest expression of the value of a single commodity.

> x commodity A = y commodity B, or
> x commodity A is worth y commodity B.

> 20 yards of linen = 1 coat, or
> 20 yards of linen are worth 1 coat.

The whole mystery of the form of value lies hidden in this elementary form. Its analysis, therefore, is our real difficulty. (48)

Here we have the turn of the first corner of the blintz:

THE FIRST CORNER OF THE BLINTZ

The Elementary or Accidental form of value

20 yards of linen = 1 coat

With what appears to be deliberate perversity, but is actually deep insight, Marx insists that we begin by abstracting even from the quantitative aspect of the elementary relationship between twenty yards of linen and one coat, concentrating simply on the assertion that some amount of linen is equal in value to some number of coats. What exactly is involved in the assertion that an amount of linen equals a number of coats?

The classical economists tell us that the assertion,

x yards of linen = y coats

expresses a *relation* between linen and coats. The relation is, in the jargon of logicians, *symmetric*, for if x yards of linen = y coats, then y coats = x yards of linen. But the classical economists are wrong, Marx insists. The assertion x yards of linen = y coats *expresses* the value of the linen in coats. That is entirely different from the statement, y coats = x yards of linen, which does not express the value of the linen at all. As Marx explains—if, indeed, such patent obfuscation can be labeled "explanation":

The value of the linen is represented as relative value, or appears in relative form. The coat officiates as equivalent, or appears in equivalent form. (48)

To grasp what Marx has in mind, we may begin by reflecting on our everyday experience of the sizes and weights of ordinary physical objects. Suppose that my baseball has rolled into a puddle of water, and I want to retrieve it without getting my feet wet. I need something about three feet long, rigid, not too heavy, and preferably long and thin, to reach over the puddle and push the ball out. My baseball bat just fills the bill, and I use it for the purpose. Being about three feet long, being rigid, being long and thin, and being not too heavy are all, in my immediate experience, properties of the bat. They are not relations between the bat and something else.

Although the length of the bat (like its weight, etc.) is a property of the bat itself, I cannot give expression to that property (or, speaking quixotically, the bat cannot give expression to its own length) merely by referring to the bat. How long is the bat? It is no help to say, "It is as long as itself." That is no doubt true, but it does not express the bat's length. To express the length of the bat, I must find some already existing measure of length, and set the bat in relation to that measure. I must say, for example, that the bat is three feet long. Perhaps I have a one-foot ruler which I use to measure the bat. I lay the ruler down along side the bat consecutively and note how many lengths of the ruler can be laid off against the bat from one end to the other. I thereby discover that the bat *is* three feet long. In this case, the *length* of the bat (one of its own properties) can find expression only by being set in relation to some other object which, in this context, is officiating as standard of length.

The ruler, meanwhile, stands all by itself as length, as the equivalent of length. It is the standard unit of length even when there is no bat or stick handy to lay it off against. But so long as it plays this role, it cannot itself express its own length. How long is a foot-ruler? One foot is hardly a satisfactory answer. We can, of course, answer "one third of a yard," but then the yardstick has become the standard of length, and has taken up the role of equivalent form of length. The foot-ruler is now able to express its length in relative form by being set in relation to the yardstick as standard of length.

The psychological shift in perception involved in considering the length of a stick first as the relative form of length and then as the equivalent form of length can be explored a bit more closely by considering the way in which we experience foreign weights and measures when we travel abroad. An American visitor to France who has never been out of the United States before will probably begin by translating prices, weights, and measures into their familiar American equivalents in order to find out how much things *really* cost, weigh, or measure. If the franc is currently exchanging at seven to the dollar, then a franc is "worth" fourteen cents, in which case a newspaper that costs two francs *really* costs twenty-eight cents. A journey of 120 kilometers is *really* 75 miles long. When the thermometer reads 30°C, it is *really* 86 degrees.

At first, if I am the traveler, I must carry out this translation in order to grasp the properties of the objects and situations I encounter. I don't know whether a restaurant is cheap or expensive until I convert its prices into dollars. So too, the one-franc piece has a certain worth, or value (for I experience it as an object having value, not as the embodiment or equivalent of value). I find out what its value is, I express its value, by ascertaining how much a one-franc coin will cost me (that is, fourteen cents).

Little by little, a network of associations develops around the franc piece, or the meter stick, or the kilometer signs. I begin to know immediately whether a five-kilometer hike is a long walk or a short one, whether I ought to blanch at spending one hundred francs for a meal, whether a prediction of a 30°C day means shorts and a T-shirt or a jacket and sweater. Eventually, I may reach a point at which I genuinely switch over to francs and kilometers and degrees centigrade, in which case the kilometer will take up, for me, the role of equivalent form of length, and the degree centigrade will become the equivalent form of temperature. In that case, when I ask how long a proposed journey is, I will conceive the journey as having a certain length, which is a property of that journey, and I will seek to express that length in terms of the equivalent form of length, namely kilometers. But I will no more experience the question about the length of the journey as an implicit question about the relation between the journey and something else than I did the original question about the length of a kilometer, back when the mile or the foot was, for me, the equivalent form of length.

Thus, statements to the effect that a stick is three feet long or that a book weighs two pounds are experienced by us as descriptions of the properties of the stick or the book, not as assertions of relationships between the stick and a foot-rule, or the book and a lead weight.

In like manner, Marx says, we experience statements about the value of a commodity as a quantitative characterization of a certain property of that commodity, namely its *value.* Marx begins with the linen and the coat in order to force us to see that what happens in that rather fatuous example is logically identical with what happens when we say, familiarly, that the linen is worth ten shillings. In the case of the coat and the linen, since neither of those commodities has, in our experience, played the role of money, it seems odd and provocative to say that the value of the linen finds expression in the body of the coat. We are not accustomed to thinking of a length of linen as being worth so many coats, any more than we are accustomed to thinking of a stick as being so many centimeters long. Hence, when Marx forces us to transform the symmetric relation between coats and linen into an expression of the value of the linen by means of the equivalent, coats, we experience his assertions as cognitively dissonant. But, Marx points out, say the same thing in terms of gold or silver and it sounds quite comfortable to the ear.

Marx develops the transition from the simple relation between linen and coats to the full-blown system of monetary exchange of commodities with exquisite slowness and detail. First, as we have seen, he analyzes the assertion, linen = coats, only then passing on to the assertion that 20 yards of linen = 1 coat. Finally, he is ready for the second corner of the blintz, which he calls the "Total or Expanded form of value." At this stage, we have as many assertions of equality between pairs of commodities as there are possible pairs to be compared. Corn and iron, potatoes and shirts, shoes and bibles, tea and silver—for each pair, there is a statement expressing the simple, particular, or accidental form of value. Thus (62):

THE SECOND CORNER OF THE BLINTZ

The Total or Expanded form of value

20 yards of linen = 1 coat or = 10 lbs. tea or = 40 lbs. coffee or = 1 quarter corn or = 2 ounces gold or = ½ ton iron or = etc.

The next step is the inversion and condensation of these pairwise comparisons so that each commodity, save one, expresses its value in the *same* commodity as equivalent. In

Marx's example (65), coats, tea, coffee, corn, gold, iron, and so forth, each express their value in a certain quantity of linen. This is the third corner of the blintz (65).

THE THIRD CORNER OF THE BLINTZ

The General form of value

1 coat	
10 lbs. of tea	
40 lbs. of coffee	
1 quarter of corn	= 20 yards of linen
2 ounces of gold	
½ a ton of iron	
x com. A., etc.	

At this point, for the first time, we as readers may begin to experience linen as truly the equivalent form of value—as money. Especially after a century of anthropological explorations among peoples who use seashells, cows, or glass beads as money, we may have sufficient flexibility of imagination to begin to *feel* linen as the equivalent form of value, in much the way that we all feel dollars or pounds or francs as money. But Marx carries the development the final step, and by transposing the linen and the gold, arrives finally, by a turn of the last corner of the blintz, at the money-form of value (69).

THE LAST CORNER OF THE BLINTZ

The Money-form

20 yards of linen =	
1 coat =	
10 lbs. of tea =	
40 lbs. of coffee =	2 ounces of gold
1 qr. of corn =	
½ a ton of iron =	
x commodity A =	

To modern readers, the effect of this twenty-page-long development is somewhat blunted by the modern-day absence of gold and silver coins from circulation. Since we do not, today, experience gold as *money,* as indisputably the equivalent form of value, "20 yards of linen = 2 ounces of gold" may strike us as not too different from "20 yards of linen = 1 coat." How much is gold selling for these days? we may find ourselves wondering, in an effort to ascertain just how much the 20 yards of linen are *worth.* But if Marx had carried the development one stage further, and transformed all of these equations into statements of the form "x yards of linen = 1 dollar," then we could respond to the text in precisely the manner required to grasp its meaning.

When the money-form of value springs fully formed from the page at the end of section three, we suddenly feel a dramatic shift of perception and response. Instead of the arcane obscurity of coats and linen, of the relative form and the equivalent form, we are confronted with the most familiar of all phenomena, a list of prices of commodities. And yet, we have passed from the esoteric to the commonplace merely by one last turn of a corner of the pancake, one last shift of the value equations over which we have been puzzling for twenty pages. The effect is to force us to recognize that there is as much mystery, as much conceptual craziness, in the familiar price tags of a retail shop as in this quasi-Hegelian exposition of the forms of value.

Let me now connect this elaborate bit of conceptual explication with the subject of the previous lecture. I left off with Marx's puzzling assertion that his very own manner of talking about the phenomena of commodity exchange is crackbrained, crazy, *verrückt.* Recall that after a lengthy, twisted, brilliant derivation of the concept of abstract labor, Marx undercuts his own discourse by saying: "When I state that coats or boots stand in a relation to linen, because it is the universal incarnation of abstract human labour, the craziness of the statement is self-evident. Nevertheless, when the producers of coats and boots compare those articles with linen, or what is the same thing, with gold and silver, as the universal equivalent, they express the relation between their own private labour and the collective labour of society in the same crazy form" (76).

I concluded my last lecture by asking, rhetorically, why Marx persists in speaking a language that he himself characterizes as crazy. We still have not formulated an answer.

Marx gives us the essential clue in the very next paragraph. "The categories of bourgeois economy," he says, "consist of such like forms. They are socially valid, hence objective forms of thought for the relations of production belonging to this historically determined mode of production, i.e. commodity production" (76). *They are socially valid, HENCE objective.* In this phrase is encapsulated Marx's revolutionary theory of the objectively crazy (or contradictory) nature of capitalist social reality, and the radically new epistemological and literary standpoint following therefrom.

What does it mean to say that crazy forms of thought are socially valid, and hence are the objective forms of thought for commodity production? Consider the concept of the commodity with which Marx begins *Capital.* As natural being, a commodity is a material object with a variety of physical, chemical, and other properties which make it more or less useful in the satisfaction of human needs. But a commodity is not, *qua* commodity, a natural object. A commodity is a quantum of value. Its natural properties are accidental and irrelevant to its true inner essence, which is the crystal of abstract homogeneous socially necessary labor that lies concealed within it.

This is an absurd notion, as should by now be obvious. But Marx insists that it is nevertheless a *socially valid* notion, and hence an objective form of thought for those participating in and theorizing about the particular social relations of production and exchange characteristic of capitalism. Let us see exactly what this means.

Economic efficiency demands that both entrepreneurs and merchants abstract entirely from the natural properties of the commodities they produce and sell, attending only to their exchange value. The prudent capitalist cannot allow his economic decisions to be influenced by his normal human responses to the accidents of his wares. The tailor in love with his worsteds is no better than a whiskey priest drunk on sacramental wine. A sensuous affection for fine cloth, lingering on from a precapitalist craft pride, may incline him to a more costly suiting than the market demand justifies. Soon he will find himself driven to the wall by rational tailors whose fingers are numb to the feel of good wool, but whose metaphysical consciousness can discern the exact quantum of value in each yard of goods.

The senses are too coarse to apprehend the miracle of self-expanding value. No mechanic, however keen his eye, can perceive in the bustle of an automatic assembly line the measure of its profitability. Only the accountants, those eremites of capitalism for whom all sensory qualities fall away to reveal the transcendent crystals of value, can discern whether a firm is earning an appropriate rate of return on the value of its invested capital. Romantic entrepreneurs, enticed by the stench and heat and fire of the blast furnaces, will soon yield place to the Pythagoreans of the market, for whom only numbers are real.

Competition standarizes commodities, substitutes abstract calculation for concrete technical judgment, stifles passions and affections that are inappropriately aroused by the natural properties of goods, and breeds up by ruthless selection a new capitalist man for whom only exchange value is real. The same historical process of development produces a mass of workers who, in the homogeneity of their culture, their mobility, and their lack of particularized skills, approximate ever closer to the inverted ideal of abstract labor. As the rational becomes real, the real becomes ever more irrational. These absurd forms of thought—the commodity as quantum of crystallized value, the worker as petty commodity producer of abstract labor—acquire social validity and hence objectivity, which is to say that successful day-to-day interaction with the world of work and consumption, of production and circulation, requires workers and capitalists to apprehend their environment, interpret their experience, and guide their actions by means of them.

But if socially valid, which is to say effective in operation and confirmed in experience, then how absurd? We have already examined Marx's mocking logical analysis of the concept of a commodity as a quantum of value, in order to demonstrate the inner logical inversions on which such a notion rests. Now we must present an historical and social account of the actual human and social damage that results from the instantiation, or social validation, of the concept.

The story is twofold, on the side of the worker and on the side of the capitalist. Subjectively, the worker as purveyor of abstract, averagely efficient labor is torn between her natural human needs and the needs of capital. Her mind and body require a graceful, rational, integrated development if she is to achieve a healthy fulfillment of her nature. But the exigencies of profitability demand the services of a neutral, adaptable labor power unencumbered by such obstructive predispositions as natural body rhythms, craft traditions, or a preference for participation in the planning, direction, and evaluation of the activity of production.

The concept of abstract labor is *socially valid* because the more fully the worker construes his actual work situation in its terms, the more successful he is, as measured by the criteria implicit in the concept itself—criteria endlessly reconfirmed by employers, fellow-workers, ministers, teachers, and even by the members of his own family. The more completely he remakes himself in the image of abstract labor, the more likely he is to get and hold a job, win the praise of those around him, and weather the periodic economic storms. This repeated social confirmation confers objective validity on the concept, so that finally it comes to seem that resistance to the regime of the machine is mulish stubbornness, rejection of the authority of the bosses is sinful rebelliousness, and dissatisfaction with a subsistence wage is self-indulgence. The absurdity, the crackbrainedness of the concept of the commodity, Marx holds, is, on the subjective side, made manifest in the increasing misery of the increasingly productive, increasingly twisted and thwarted, ever more alienated workers.

On the objective side, on the side of capital, the immediate and irrefutable evidences of the absurdity of the categories of bourgeois political economy are the periodic crises that threaten to bring to a disastrous halt the processes of reproduction and accumulation. Economic crises, Marx argues, are the direct consequence of the attempt by capitalists to conform their economic decisions to the tenets of rationality enshrined in the socially valid, and hence objective, categories of bourgeois political economy. It is the social relations of production and circulation, not the technology of capitalism, that produce crises. The self-destructiveness of capitalism results naturally from the capitalists' reduction of all economic decisions to profitability, to the quantitative measurement of self-expanding value. The concepts of value, money, and capital achieve social validity through their short-term success. Capitalists unable or unwilling to live by the ascetic rule of profit-maximization are driven to the wall in the competition of the market. The craziness of these concepts is manifested in the crises that periodically destroy even the most economically rational of entrepreneurs.

Thus we see that there is an inner theoretical connection between Marx's economic doctrines of exploitation and crisis, his psychological theory of alienation, and his metaphysical thesis of the objective irrationality of capitalist social formations.

Marx's philosophical, as opposed to his economic, doctrines have often been construed in ways that make them relatively impervious to disconfirmation. It is important therefore to observe that if this reading of Marx is correct, then the soundness of his philosophical conception of the objective irrationality of capitalism depends essentially both on his claim that capitalism produces a progressive alienation of the working class, and on the thesis that capitalism is fatally prone to evermore serious economic crises. If the evidence leads us to give up these hypotheses, then we lose the critical perspective from which we can issue a negative evaluation of capitalism. But, of course, that is the price of nonvacuous theory.

Throughout these pages, I have been scattering promissory notes entitling the bearer to an explanation of the relationship between ontology and literary style in Marx's *Capital*. The time has come to make good on at least some of those notes.

Recall my opening remarks in the first of these lectures. The language in which a social theory finds expression, I argued, must be adequate, in its linguistic resources, to the ontological structure of the object of its discourse. The classical political economists believed that capitalism as such is a rational form of economic organization. It is the people living in a capitalist society who sometimes fall short of that objective rationality, by failing to guide their investments, purchases, sales, and public tax policies by prudentially rational calculation. The subjective irrationality of economic agents leads in turn to economic distortions, and thence even to economic crises. Consequently, Ricardo and his school use a transparent prose designed to reveal the objective rational economic structure lying beneath the sometimes confusing surface appearances of market prices, temporary super-profits, and local customs. We, as readers, are encouraged thereby to adjust our subjective performances to the objective rationality of capitalism.

But Marx, as we now see, holds that capitalism is objectively irrational. The central irrationalities may be summarized under four headings:

First, the human capacity for productive laboring is treated as a commodity to be bought and sold in the market for a price. Indeed, as Marx and Engels show us in their vivid factual accounts of the condition of wage-laborers under early capitalism, mothers and fathers actually produced this capacity for laboring, as embodied in their children, in order that it might be sold on the market at the reduced wages assigned to child labor.

Second, in a capitalist economy, production is carried out for the purpose of making a profit, not for the purpose of satisfying human needs, with the consequence that desires must be artificially created for profitable commodities while basic human wants go unsatisfied.

Third, under capitalism, economic relationships appear to

us in mystified form as a network of mutually beneficial exchanges of equals for equals, whereas in fact capitalism is a structure of exploitation of workers by capitalists.

And finally, political economy represents produced goods and services, through the mediation of market exchange and the system of money, in crackpot metaphysical fashion as quanta of abstract value clothed in sensory garb.

To talk about this world, Marx finds, the transparent, one-dimensional language of the classical school is thoroughly inadequate, indeed, directly misleading. As I observed in my second lecture, he needs a language whose syntactic and tropic resources are rich enough to permit him to accomplish a number of literary and theoretical ends simultaneously.

To begin with, the language of Marx's discourse must permit him to represent the quantitative relationships that actually obtain in capitalist production and exchange. In other words, it must be a language and a set of concepts with which he can formulate a satisfactory theory of price. Many of the modern students of Marx who come to him from the disciplines of philosophy, literature, or political science fail to recognize the absolute necessity of this first requirement. Puzzled, or else discouraged, by the complexities of the classical theory of natural price, these readers allow themselves to imagine that Marx's vision of capitalism can be rendered in purely qualitative and social-psychological terms. But Marx himself knew better. Only an account of capitalism that establishes with quantitative precision the locus and magnitude of exploitation can hope to accomplish the destructive critique that Marx thought himself to have devised.

Furthermore, while revealing the quantitative determination of prices, wages, and profits, and thereby the underlying structure of exploitation, the language of *Capital* must permit critics like Marx to articulate the structure of mystification that conceals the exploitative and self-destructive character of capitalism. It must be possible, in this language, not merely to state a theory of price alongside a theory of mystification, but actually to capture linguistically the way in which the mystifications of value and equal exchange serve as the necessary surface appearance of the underlying structure of exploitation.

In addition, as we learned from our reflections on the case of Socrates, the language of political economy must serve to implicate the speaker in the very patterns of mystification that are being exposed. It must be a language that can express a self-understanding of our own false consciousness, and of the degree to which we have managed to liberate ourselves therefrom.

And finally, this language cannot be entirely self-contained in its scope of theoretical applicability. It must offer the resources for an eventual transcendence of the mystifications of the capitalist market.

All this, I suggest, Marx sought to accomplish by means of the ironic discourse of the opening chapters of *Capital.* Writing for an audience that had been reared on the mysteries and incantations of Christianity, he invoked its most powerful metaphors to force upon his readers a self-awareness of their complicity in the inversions and fetishism of capitalist market relations. By "coquetting with Hegel," as he himself described his discussion of the concepts of value and money, Marx clearly hoped to jolt the complacent apologists of capitalism into a realization of the opacity, mystery, and underlying irrationality of their putatively transparent explanations of prices, wages, and profits.

If I am correct in my reading of *Capital,* then we must reject, or at least significantly reinterpret, Marx's oft-repeated claim that *his* political economy, in contradistinction to that of so many of his predecessors, was scientific. In advancing that claim, Marx clearly had two contrasts in mind, both of which, I think, are sustained by my reading of the text. First, he meant to counterpose his work to that of the utopian socialists, who, he thought, conjured their fantasies of a better world with little or no analysis of the structure of capitalism and the roots of exploitation. Second, he wished to contrast his work, and that of selected authors such as Ricardo, to the superficial apologetics of the post-Ricardians whom he stigmatized as vulgar economists. Scientific political economy penetrated the surface appearances to reveal the objective structure of exploitation underneath, whereas vulgar economy, like the pseudoscience of the denizens of Plato's cave, merely contented itself with predicting the flicker of the shadows on the wall.

Clearly, Marx is right to insist that *his* enterprise be disassociated both from utopian dreaming and vulgar apologetics. But in another, more modern, sense of the term "scientific" Marx is wrong about his own enterprise, and indeed about social analysis and critique in general. Precisely because Marx's vision of capitalist society requires for its expression an ironic authorial voice, *Capital* is not, in the modern acceptation, a scientific work. Its insights and revelations are imperfectly rendered by a textbook redaction of the theory of surplus value or the thesis of the tendency of the rate of profit to fall. Like a great novel, a great work of social theory is an inherently perspectival rendering of an authorial vision. Its truth as well as its power resides at least in part in the ironic implication of its author in the mystifications and injustices that it exposes.

It is for this reason that we continue to read *Capital* more than a century after its publication. And it is for this reason, as well, that we who aspire to follow Marx's path must struggle to find for ourselves a voice in which to speak of the inversions, the mystifications, the *verrücktheit,* of our own age.